D0373443

Sagebrush Country
A Wildflower Sanctuary

Ronald J. Taylor

Mountain Press Publishing Company
1992

Copyright © 1992
Ronald J. Taylor

Cover painting by Mary Beth Percival

Drawings by Trudi Peek

Library of Congress Cataloging-in-Publication Data

Taylor, Ronald J., 1932-
    Sagebrush country : a wildflower sanctuary / Ronald J. Taylor. —
[Rev. ed.]
        p.   cm.
    Includes index.
    ISBN 0-87842-280-3   : $12.00
    1. Wild flowers—Great Basin—Identification.   I. Title.
QK141.T39   1992   92-13520
582. 13'0979—dc20   CIP

Printed in Hong Kong by Mantec Production Company

Mountain Press Publishing Company
2016 Strand Avenue • P.O. Box 2399
Missoula, MT 59801
(406) 728-1900

This book is dedicated to George G. Taylor (father of the author), who was born, played, worked, and died within the limits of the sagebrush steppe. He was a man who appreciated the varied beauty and tranquility of nature, a man who loved the great outdoors as he loved life itself.

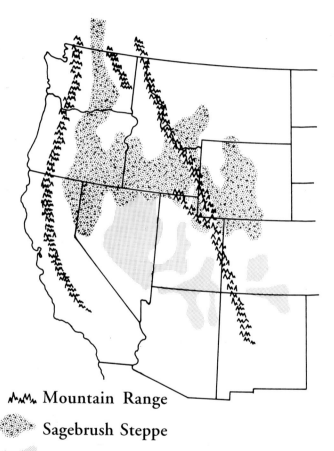

ᴬᴠᴹᴠ Mountain Range

Sagebrush Steppe

Great Basin Sagebrush "Desert"

Sagebrush Country

Contents

Acknowledgements

In completing this work, I have referred extensively to various floras and other botanical treatments dealing with the plants growing in sagebrush country. As much as possible, I have relied on the comprehensive flora *Vascular Plants of the Pacific Northwest* (vol. 1-5) by Hitchcock, Cronquist, Ownbey, and Thompson as the primary authority on plant descriptions and distribution. Among the numerous scientists who have contributed toward an understanding of the ecology and floristics of the sagebrush steppe, Rexford Daubenmire deserves special recognition. He spent a career studying and describing the communities of sagebrush country. The knowledge I have gained from that great teacher has contributed information to and influenced the orientation of this book. I gratefully acknowledge Ira Spring for taking some of the animal photographs herein and thank him for his generosity in allowing me to use them. Finally, I would like to acknowledge the involvement and coauthorship of Rolf Valum in a previous edition of this book. Rolf and I spent many pleasant days photographing wildflowers in sagebrush country.

Mosaic of spring flowers—prairie lupine, arrow-leaf balsamroot, and showy phlox.

Prologue

Sagebrush country is a land of contrasts, a place of desolation or a place of beauty. It may appear as a lifeless, lonely wilderness or an ecosystem teeming with insects, vertebrates, and plant life. The cold winters bring biting wind and blowing snow; summer days are uncomfortably hot but pass rather quickly into cool nights beneath clear, starry skies. Because of the winter cold and summer drought, a large part of the sagebrush zone has been called a cold desert. Still, occasional thunderstorms drench the cracked soil and rejuvenate the dormant plant life.

The landscape is equally diverse—sandy plains and alkaline flats rise to rugged rocky cliffs and steep mountain slopes. The topography largely determines the nature of the soil by influencing wind and erosional patterns, creating deep and fertile soils in areas of deposition and shallow and rocky soils in windblown and eroded areas.

To many people sagebrush country is a wasteland, a dusty world of sand and tumbleweeds separating the scattered towns of the West that represent civilization. To others sagebrush country presents a fantasyland rich in legend and romanticism of the American cowboy of storybook and celluloid fame. Yet, real beauty exists here for those who seek it, beauty expressed in colorful spring and fall flowers and more subtly in the wondrous adaptations that enable plants and animals to withstand the extremes so typical of the sagebrush steppe. There is also enjoyment in being a part of sagebrush country, in camping under the stars with the ever-present smell of sage, listening for the eerie howl of the ubiquitous coyote, and being keenly aware of one's "aloneness" in these wide open spaces. Sadly, the sagebrush steppe has dwindled in size and quality with the advancement of the plow and increased availability of irrigational water, and the wide abuse by various special interest groups. In much of the West, the steppe persists only in islands unsuitable for other uses. Perhaps 25% of the original steppe persists, much of it badly altered. Fortunately, The Nature Conservancy and other private and public agencies are now attempting to preserve remnants of the various steppe ecosystems.

The sagebrush steppe in northern Nevada

Great Basin sagebrush desert in late winter

Introduction

Sagebrush country, as treated in this book, includes the sagebrush steppe and the Great Basin sagebrush desert—a territory that covers most of Nevada, northeastern California, eastern Oregon and Washington, southern Idaho, southwestern Montana, much of Utah, western Wyoming and the foothills and valleys of northwestern Colorado. For convenience, I refer to sagebrush country inclusively as the sagebrush steppe or simply the steppe. Sagebrush itself extends well beyond these rather arbitrary bounds, however, and may dominate local plant communities on the relatively moist northern slopes of desert mountains in California and the southern Rockies or on the winter-chilled, wind-swept plains of western Canada. Although this book does not characterize these outlying communities nor include pictures and descriptions of associated plants found there, the vegetation resembles that of the steppe proper.

The accompanying map illustrates the rather arbitrary limits of sagebrush country. However, within these limits, sagebrush-dominated communities are highly fragmented as a result of climate, topography, and various human activities, especially agricultural development.

I have used the community concept rather extensively in this book. A community is a more or less repeatable association of dominant and subordinate plants, plants that you will consistently find growing together in similar habitat. Dominants are those plants that exert the greatest influence on the community because of their size and/or density. Subordinates are simply associates; they have adapted to the same habitat as the dominant plants but play a somewhat less conspicuous role in the community. The name of the community normally reflects the dominant species. For example, a common community type of the bunchgrass prairie (eastern Washington and Oregon and much of Idaho) is *Agropyron spicatum / Artemisia tridentata* (bluebunch wheatgrass/tall sagebrush). Subordinates include any one or combination of most plants listed under the standard type zone of the sagebrush steppe.

Sagebrush communities are indeed very widespread in the American West, but they are much more limited in distribution than may be apparent. Upon casual observation from a speeding vehicle, many shrubs of the steppes

1

and deserts closely resemble sagebrush. Regularly spaced shrubs with low, symmetrical profiles constitute a major part of the dominant vegetation from the Mojave Desert north through the sagebrush steppe and east into southern Utah and Colorado. Many of these plants are sagebrush "look-alikes," not the real thing.

Another problem with defining the limits of the sagebrush steppe or identifying sagebrush communities pertains to other often very closely related species of Artemisia, the genus that contains true sagebrush. If the *Artemisia* species as a group are considered to be sagebrush, then sagebrush in the broad sense becomes more widely distributed and ecologically more diverse. This book treats sagebrush more or less in the broad sense, but certainly *Artemisia tridentata*, tall sagebrush, is the most widespread, the most common, and the most ecologically important of the several species.

Considerable vegetative diversity exists over the vast geographical area of the sagebrush steppe. In the Great Basin, sagebrush-dominated communities overlap extensively with the more drought-tolerant vegetation, such as species of *Atriplex* (shadscale or saltbrush), of the northern, upland extension of the Mojave Desert—a region that supports relatively simple plant communities with few conspicuous dominants and sparse associated species. In the foothills and high plains, the sagebrush steppe contacts and becomes interspersed with woodland communities—piñon pine and juniper in the south, juniper and/or mountain mahogany or gambels oak in the north and east. In some areas, particularly in Idaho and Washington, the sagebrush steppe interfingers with ponderosa pine and Douglas fir forests. Here the transition between forest and steppe is abrupt with isolated sagebrush communities growing on dry, south-facing slopes in otherwise forested regions. At the higher and northern limits of the sagebrush steppe, soil moisture is more readily available and consequently the associated vegetation tends to grow very lush with numerous representative species. Over this broad steppeland region of western North America—variable in climate, topography, and species—the single most important unifying characteristic is the presence of sagebrush, usually conspicuous and often dominant.

VEGETATIVE ZONES

Within a given area, such as the sagebrush steppe, the vegetation follows a pattern of distribution or zonation determined in large part by the physical and chemical properties of the soil. This book recognizes six vegetative zones, an over-simplification that keeps the subject manageable. These zones are by no means absolute and the distribution of species within them is inconsistent from location to location. Still, each zone represents a pattern of vegetative uniformity both in species and plant form, and it is possible to relate most of the steppeland species to one or more of these six zones.

Standard-type zone — The standard-type zone is characterized by a lack of extremes. The soil is moderately deep, somewhat sandy and/ or gravelly, usually slightly alkaline, and sufficiently moist to

Piñon-juniper community, Mt. Jefferson (Oregon) as backdrop

Gambels oak—sagebrush transition in Uinta Mountains, Utah

support tall sagebrush (*Artemisia tridentata*) and various grasses, the zone's two most prevalent plant types. In the more moist sites, particularly near forest margins, bitterbrush (*Purshia tridentata*) communities are representative, with associates that commonly include sagebrush, grasses, lupines, and balsamroots (*Balsamorhiza* species). In somewhat drier sandy sites, species of rabbit brush (*Chrysothamnus*) are extremely common with associates similar to those of the bitterbrush communities. Other conspicuous dominants of the standard-type zone include several species of desert buckwheat (*Eriogonum*). Less common but colorful associates include species of Indian paintbrush (*Castilleja*), penstemon (*Penstemon*), larkspur (*Delphinium*), phlox (*Phlox*), desert parsley (*Lomatium*), locoweed (*Astragalus*), several daisies (*Erigeron*), and various liliaceous plants including wild onions (*Allium*), death camas (*Zygadenus*), and wild hyacinths (*Brodiaea*).

The standard-type zone is by far the most productive of the various vegetative zones (meadows excluded). Much of this zone is under cultivation, particularly areas with irrigable, deep soil. Most of the remainder is utilized to varying degrees for livestock grazing. Extreme grazing pressure allows weedy, less palatable plant species to replace the natural vegetation. Unfortunately much of the sagebrush steppe has been overgrazed and thus altered, in some cases irreversibly so.

Lithosol zone — Lithosol literally means rock-soil. Most lithosols develop in areas underlain by basalt, a dark volcanic rock. Soil deposition is insignificant and primarily restricted to cracks in the basalt. Yet, because of the undesirable environmental conditions, rather than in spite of them, the lithosols provide some of the most spectacular arrays of spring flowers to be found in the sagebrush steppe. The more competitive plants, such as tall sagebrush and dominant grasses, cannot withstand the rigors of the lithosols and, therefore, do not crowd out the less competitive but more environmentally tolerant lithosol species. Most lithosol species grow close to the ground and resemble the cushion plants of the arctic and alpine tundra. This adaptation provides the plants with protection against extreme water loss in the hot sun and drying wind. Water is, of course, a major growth-limiting factor in the lithosol zone; by midsummer the plants have become dormant showing few signs of life. The most important species of lithosols are stiff sagebrush (*Artemisia rigida*), desert buckwheat (*Eriogonum*), and dwarf goldenweed (*Haplopappus acaulis*). Common, showy spring flowering associates include cushion phlox (*Phlox hoodii*), rock penstemon (*Penstemon gairdneri*), daisies and other members of the sunflower family, and a few cacti. Low grasses also grow as subordinates.

Sagebrush–Bunchgrass community, Richland, Washington

Balsamroot and Lupine

Bitterbrush–Lupine community

Stiff sagebrush community with yellow daisies along the Columbia River near Vantage, Washington

Dune with sagebrush

Sand (dune) zone — The soil of the sagebrush steppe tends to be sandy, often obscuring the distinction between a dune area and the more sandy element of the standard-type zone. Still the distinction does exist as reflected by the representative vegetation. In the dune zone, the sand tends to move, creating an unstable environment that selects for those plants that can tolerate shifts in sand depth. These plants normally grow on horizontal stems that produce upright shoots, or they regenerate from lateral buds as the sand deposition increases. dune areas characteristically are deficient in nitrogen. Therefore, only plants that can provide (or fix) their own nitrogen, such as lupines and other legumes, or those which can tolerate nitrogen deficiencies become established here. Sand inhabitants of the latter group include sand dock (*Rumex venosus*), white-stemmed primrose (*Oenothera pallida*), Indian rice grass (*Oryzopsis hymenoides*), and a number of short-lived annuals such as dwarf purple monkey flower (*Mimulus nanus*). As the sand becomes more stabilized, rabbit brush and other "sand-loving" species of the standard-type zone establish themselves, providing a mixture of vegetation from the two intergrading zones.

Talus zone — Numerous rocky outcrops, hills, and canyons punctuate the sagebrush steppe. The slopes of many of these topographic irregularities are covered with coarse gravel or boulders. These talus slopes tend to be unstable, and this favors a particular combination of plants, mostly large shrubs such as serviceberry (*Amelanchier alnifolia*) and squaw currant (*Ribes cereum*). Fine graveled talus supports a number of small, low shrubs (or subshrubs) including the beautiful and conspicuous purple sage (*Salvia dorrii*), Oregon sunshine (*Eriophyllum Lanatum*), penstemon, desert buckwheat (*Eriogonum*), and evening primrose (*Oenothera*). Most talus shrubs, particularly the larger ones, require comparatively large amounts of water, which they get from channeled drainage of precipitation through the rock system. As the establishment of vegetation, splintering of rocks, and deposition of wind-blown soil begin to stabilize a talus slope, many herbaceous species, such as lupines, invade the area to develop a lush community of mixed vegetation. This slow process of geological and vegetational change ultimately results in the conversion to a standard-type soil zone; the dominant sagebrush and grasses establish themselves and subsequently eliminate most talus species.

Meadow zone — In the high sagebrush plains, the drainage pattern causes meadows to form in low depressions. These meadows are, of course, wet year-round. The vegetation contrasts sharply with that of drier sites and includes many species of sedge (*Carex*), rushes (Juncus), some grasses, and a few very attractive flowering plants such as wild iris (*Iris*) and camas (*Camasia*). Various willows (*Salix*)

The meadow in the center is dominated by sedges and willows, near Leadore, Idaho.

Greasewood playa

usually grow in or around meadows, often forming dense thickets that provide shelter for wildlife. Seepage areas also support a very restricted and meadow-like vegetative community. These seeps develop most frequently along rock ledges below forests and provide a brilliant rock-garden-like display of wildflowers. Some of the most common and widespread representatives of these seepages are yellow monkey flower (*Mimulus guttatus*), shooting star (*Dodecatheon*), a number of wild saxifrages, and naked broomrape (*Orobanche uniflora*), a root parasite on the saxifrages.

Saline zone — As rocks weather they release calcium carbonates, sodium salts, and other alkaline compounds. In areas of low precipitation, these compounds are not leached from the soil but accumulate to produce somewhat saline soils. If the parent rock is especially rich in soluble salts, the soil becomes so saline that only salt-tolerant species can grow. These plants, called halophytes, contain high internal concentrations of salts, which allows them to withdraw water from salty soils; other plants cannot do this and would perish from dehydration. Most salt-tolerant plants are non-showy shrubs of the Goosefoot family (*Chenopodiaceae*), and the most common representatives in the sagebrush steppe are hop sage (*Atriplex spinosa*), winterfat (*Eurotia lanata*), and greasewood (*Sarcobatus vermiculatus*). In many parts of the steppe, the water table lies near the surface and shallow ponds or lakes form during wet periods. The water slowly evaporates leaving a salty residue. These low areas, termed playas or saltflats, are inhabited by a few extremely salt-tolerant species that include saltbush or shadscale (*Atriplex species*), greasewood, and saltgrass (*Distichylis stricta*).

ADAPTATIONS

Since water essentially limits plant growth and reproduction in the sagebrush steppe, the plants have evolved a combination of adaptations that enable them to cope with drought. These numerous and varied adaptations fall into three general categories: (1) those that enable plants to tolerate drought; (2) those that assist the plants in avoiding drought; and (3) those that enable plants to escape drought altogether.

Adaptations leading to drought tolerance are physiological in nature and occur in a few desert species. Some enable plant tissue to become extremely dehydrated without permanent cell damage—vital water may be bound in cytoplasmic colloids; others allow plants to extract water from very dry soil—the plants develop a very negative osmotic potential (water sucking potential) as a result of internal salt concentrations.

Plants avoid drought through structural modifications that enable them to retain or conserve water. Common adaptations of this type include: (1) a thick waxy coating, or cuticle, on the stems and leaves that helps retain moisture;

9

Sagebrush steppe, northern Nevada

(2) hairiness, or pubescence, which reduces evaporation from leaf surfaces by inhibiting air movement across the leaves and by reflecting sunlight, thus having a cooling effect; (3) the ability to store water in the plant's tissue, a condition called succulence, which provides vital moisture during periods of drought; 4) low ratio of leaf surface to leaf volume, exemplified by small thick leaves, round leaves, rolled leaves, or folded leaves, all modifications that cut down on evaporative surface area; and 5) various modifications of internal leaf anatomy that help to reduce loss of water vapor, or transpiration, and that guard against structural leaf damage resulting from excessive wilting.

Plants that escape drought either have a persistent water supply or carry out their entire life cycle during the moist time of year. The latter group of plants, called annuals, are extremely common in the steppe. They survive the dry periods as seeds.

THE WHYS AND WHEREFORES OF PLANT NAMES

Humans are rational animals who consciously or subconsciously strive to eliminate disorganization and confusion from life. This has naturally led to the categorization and naming of all manner of things, since a name is necessary for efficient communication. Problems of communication continue to exist, however, since names tend to be regional. The broader the distribution of a species, the greater the number of common names applied to that species. In an attempt to eliminate the ambiguities of common names, botanists have adopted a set of rules and regulations leading to acceptance of a single name for each species. This scientific or Latin name actually consists of two names: the genus and the specific epithet. Still, communication problems persist because of the inability to identify with a foreign sounding name that usually has no obvious meaning. Considering these difficulties, I have used common names extensively in this book, with Latin names providing accuracy of identification. I must emphasize, however, that many of the more colorful and widespread species have several common names. I have made an attempt to use the most widely recognized common name or names.

What is in a name? The Latin binomial, the species, consists of a noun (the genus or generic name) and a descriptive adjective (the specific epithet). The generic name may be descriptive in nature or it may be given in honor of a person or place. Many originated in antiquity, especially with the ancient Greeks. The specific epithet, although generally descriptive, may also honor a person or place, in which case it takes an adjectival form. Thus, there is meaning in the Latin binomial. It is descriptive and informative but, unfortunately, only to individuals with knowledge of Latin and an appreciation for ancient Greek, ancient Roman, and early American history. It is not surprising, therefore, that people tend to be "turned-off" by Latin names and instead use common names that serve the same function on a regional scale. Such names may be descriptive, as yellowbell or tumbleweed; they may relate to a habitat or location, such as desert paintbrush or Oregon sunshine; or they may have seasonal or diurnal significance, such as spring beauty and evening primrose. Some names—winterfat, for instance—reflect a use. Finally, many common names are direct translations of the Latin, such as "balsamroot" from *Balsamorhiza.*

POLLINATION STRATEGIES OF STEPPE WILDFLOWERS

Coadaptations Between Plants and Their Insect Pollinators

The shape, size, color, and odor of flowers is not arbitrary. These characteristics dictate the mode of pollination or the pollination strategy. The coadaptation between a flower and its pollinator is a fine-tuned phenomenon that ensures successful reproduction and survival. In simpler terms, the plant conditions the insect by providing a food reward, usually nectar and/or pollen. The insect associates various floral features, as those noted above, with a reward and seeks out flowers of other plants of the same species. The result is successful pollination.

Pollination strategies fall into four very general categories: fly/beetle, bee, butterfly/moth, and wind. Flies and/or beetles pollinate "generalist" types of flowers: usually bowl-shaped, with radial symmetry, no fusion of parts, and easily accessible rewards (nectar and/or pollen). The pollinators walk around on the flowers in a seemingly haphazard manner getting dusted with pollen—a process sometimes called "mess and soil" pollination. Typical generalist flowers of the sagebrush steppe are sagebrush buttercup, bitterroot, and spring beauty.

Butterfly and moth flowers have floral tubes that conceal the nectar and require a long tongue to reach it. The tube normally forms through the fusion of petals. The flowers are typically radially symmetrical, trumpet shaped, and pastel-colored or white. Examples of butterfly/moth flowers of the sagebrush steppe include phlox, collomia, evening primrose, and some members of the sunflower (aster) family.

Bees, especially bumblebees, pollinate highly specialized, usually bilaterally symmetrical flowers with a well-marked landing pad and nectar guides. Petals are often fused into a tube with the stamens and stigma precisely positioned for certain pollination. The nectar is concealed at the base of the floral tube. Bees use a combination of shape, color, and odor to recognize a chosen flower. They alight on the pad and move into the "gullet" of the floral tube, directed by the colorful nectar guides. In the process, the stamens precisely position the pollen on the bee, to be deposited on the stigma of the next flower visited. Frequently the "clever" bee has to manipulate the flower to gain access to the floral tube. Among bee-pollinated plants of the steppe are penstemons and sagebrush violet. Bees, however, are opportunists and visit nearly all types of flowers.

Beetle on cow parsnip (a meadow species)

Syrphid fly on spring beauty

Bumblebee on wild onion

Wind-pollinated flowers are small and inconspicuous, usually lacking colorful parts—they need not advertise for their pollinator. The stamens and stigmas extend outward into the wind stream. The large anthers produce massive amounts of pollen, and the usually feathery stigma combs the air stream to collect it. The flowers are often unisexual. Many of the dominant plants of the sagebrush steppe are wind-pollinated, including sagebrush and grasses.

ANIMALS OF THE SAGEBRUSH STEPPE

The survival of many of the animals historically associated with "sagebrush country"—such as the black-footed ferret, prairie chicken, and prairie falcon—is threatened by wholesale habitat destruction. Even the prairie dog, known for its expansive colonies, now inhabits just a few scattered locations. However, most of the steppe residents show amazing resilience and continue to thrive in the face of adversity. Among the latter are the coyote, jackrabbit, antelope, rattlesnake, and ground squirrel.

Regardless of their abundance, animals all have their special combination of adaptive characteristics—physical, physiological, and behavioral—that enable them to survive in the hostile world of the sagebrush steppe. A variety of strategies enable them to escape humans and other predators. Many animals, such as sage grouse and the ornate horned toad (lizard), depend on

Badger —*Ira Spring photo*

Antelope —*Ira Spring photo*

Horned lizard

Sage grouse

allusiveness and camouflage. The antelope and jackrabbit use speed and alertness. The inquisitive ground squirrel and quarrelsome badger escape into burrows. And some, such as the wily coyote, depend on quick wit.

To deal with the heat and drought of summer, most animals restrict their activity to early morning and evening; some, such as the ground squirrel enter into a period of aestivation—light hibernation—during the summer drought. The winters are much more difficult to deal with. Some animals, especially birds, migrate to warmer climes; some, such as rodents, hibernate. Most "don" their winter coats or feathers, seek shelter during the storms, and simply tough it out. Most insects survive the winter as eggs, deposited in protected sites. Perhaps the most hazardous period for insects is early spring when it can be "balmy" during the day but freezing at night. Many insects are protected from the cold by "antifreeze" in their blood. Some insects, such as bumblebees and hawkmoths, are able to heat their muscles by vibration, thus remaining active during cold periods. This, of course, expends much energy. The bees and moths can conserve energy, however, by heating only their flight muscles and tolerating cold rear ends and feet.

How To Use This book

This book contains a broad selection, though not all, of the most common, attractive, or otherwise interesting plants of the sagebrush steppe. Plant families are arranged alphabetically by common name, with the scientific name for the family provided. This arrangement will be convenient for persons who are familiar with the various families. Those people who lack this familiarity—for whom one organizational method is probably as good (or as bad) as another—will at least get some idea of the relationships among families. Individual plants (species) are also arranged according to relationships within families. An exception to this is sagebrush which, although in the sunflower family (Compositae), comes first in the descriptive section, apart from its family. The ecological importance of sagebrush in the steppes of North America and its inclusion in the title of this book justifies this special treatment.

The identification of an unknown plant can probably be made by searching through the photographs of a likely family, if the plant has been included in this book. The associated description will help confirm this identification, as well as adding other interesting information about the plant and its habitat.

A family key (Appendix I) will assist in the identification of steppe plants. This key has been kept as simple as possible, but its usage requires recognition of major plant parts and their variant forms. Reference to the labeled illustrations and glossary will help in this respect. Keys for the identification of individual species have not been provided because they would necessarily be rather technical, and the plants included in this book represent a small percentage of those growing in the sagebrush steppe.

Appendix II, which groups species according to the vegetative zone(s) in which they most frequently occur, may also be helpful in the identification of species or may otherwise be of interest to the reader. In the index, species are listed alphabetically by common and scientific name.

SAGEBRUSH
Sunflower family

Artemisia **species**
Compositae

The term sagebrush refers collectively to several species of low shrubs distributed throughout the semiarid regions of North America. Among these species, tall sagebrush (*Artemisia tridentata*), the state flower of Nevada, has the broadest ecological tolerance and can survive under the greatest range of environmental conditions. Still, it grows best in deep, relatively moist soils that are mildly basic (rather than acidic). Under such ideal conditions, individual plants may become very large and robust, up to eight feet tall and equally broad through the branched crown. As soil conditions deteriorate and water availability decreases, tall sagebrush grows progressively smaller and in many dry, rocky areas may average less than one foot in height.

Tall sagebrush has evolved a number of adaptations "designed" to increase the efficiency of water absorption and retention under semiarid conditions. The plants produce two types of leaves. The principal, lobed ones persist throughout the year. Smaller and softer, non-lobed leaves appear along the branch tips in early winter and drop during drought conditions the following summer. This allows more rapid growth during the relatively moist conditions of early spring and enables the plant to conserve resources during the hot, dry summer. Both leaf types are small with a limited surface area from which water can be lost through evaporation (transpiration). A dense covering of grayish hairs on the leaves further reduces transpiration by reflecting sunlight, thereby cooling the plant, and by inhibiting the movement of drying wind across the leaf surface. The plants become somewhat dormant during the drier part of the year (when the soft leaves drop), thus conserving water. Tall sagebrush has an efficient two-component root system: small, widely dispersed, shallow roots absorb water rapidly before it can evaporate following rain storms; and coarse, penetrating roots draw water from reservoirs deep underground.

Although tall sagebrush has a broad ecological tolerance, it is not necessarily a strong competitor. In the more moist extremes of its ecological range it tends to be replaced by grasses and/or other shrubs, or even trees. However, the decay of its fallen leaves releases toxic compounds that apparently limit the growth of some would-be competitors. Other environmental factors also influence competitive ability. Heavy grazing depresses competing grasses and enhances sagebrush growth. In contrast, fire selectively destroys the dry, woody sagebrush plants, favoring increased density of grasses.

The minute flowers of sagebrush form numerous small yellowish heads during late summer or early fall. Although insect pollination tends to be the rule in most members of the sunflower family (Compositae), sagebrush is wind pollinated. The pollen carried on summer breezes causes an allergic response and associated discomfort in some people, further aggravated by the extended flowering period. The volatile chemicals responsible for the strong sage odor may also have a mild allergenic effect.

Tall sagebrush *Artemisia tridentata*

Among the most important identifying characteristics of tall sagebrush are leaf shape and color. The grayish color and dense hairs are distinctive. The principal leaves are wedge-shaped and three-lobed (or three-toothed as the name "tridentata" indicates) at the broadened tip.

Another important sagebrush species of the western steppeland (Washington, Oregon, Idaho, and Montana) is **stiff sagebrush (Artemisia rigida)**, a major dominant in dry, rocky (lithosol) areas. This low shrub grows up to two feet tall with deeply divided (rather than lobed) leaves and blackish stems and branches.

The genus was named in honor of Artemisia, wife of Mausolus, ancient ruler of Caria (Southwest Asia Minor). Mausolus died in 353 B.C. and his bereaved wife perpetuated his memory by erecting a magnificent mausoleum which became one of the seven wonders of the world. Artemisia herself was named in honor of the Greek goddess Artemis, the virgin huntress or goddess of wild nature.

Stiff sagebrush *Artemisia rigida*

BORAGE FAMILY Boraginaceae

A combination of characteristics easily distinguishes borage from other families. The flower cluster, or inflorescence, is typically coiled (scorpioid); stiff hairs usually cover the entire plant; the petals are fused into a narrow tube with five spreading petal lobes; and the ovary matures into four one-seeded nutlets. The borage family is large and well represented in the sagebrush steppe.

Bluebell *Mertensia longiflora*

The beautiful, early-flowering bluebell is fairly common in areas of abundant spring moisture in the high plains of the steppe and in open coniferous forests. This rather succulent plant has branched tuberous roots, six- to eight-inch stems, and leathery, bluish leaves that broaden toward the tip. Each plant produces one to several leafy stems with densely packed nodding or drooping flowers. The petals are fused into a tube with an expanded, lobed tip, and they separate very easily from the rest of the flower. The nodding blooms and tubular petals give the flowers a bell-like appearance. The sky blue or darker flowers often fade to pinkish with age.

Bluebells grow most frequently beneath sagebrush "canopies" and in other sheltered sites in the western expanse of the steppeland.

Cryptantha *Cryptantha* species

Cryptantha is a rather large genus with several species represented in the sagebrush steppe, including annual, biennial, and perennial herbs. Most are small (less than 18 inches tall), coarsely hairy or bristly plants with rather inconspicuous flowers. The small white or rarely yellow petals are fused into a tube with five spreading lobes. Bristly-hairy sepals often more-or-less hide the petals.

The most attractive cryptanthas are erect perennials with tightly packed flower clusters and many basal, non-lobed leaves. Two of the showiest white-flowered species are *Cryptantha glomerata*, a common plant of sandy and gravelly sites in Wyoming, Utah, and Colorado, and *C. leucophylla*, a sand-loving species of eastern Washington and adjacent Oregon. The most attractive of all cryptanthas is the bright yellow-flowered *C. flava*, which frequently inhabits sandy plains of the Great Basin.

Bluebell *Mertensia longiflora*

Cryptantha *Cryptantha glomerata*

Cryptantha *Cryptantha flava*

23

Puccoon

Lithospermum ruderale

This rather unattractive herb sports a large cluster of leafy stems derived from a strong woody root. The narrow leaves are one to four inches long, the lower ones even smaller. The dull pale yellow or greenish flowers grow partially hidden among the numerous leaves near the stem tip. The petals are fused at the base into a narrow tube with five spreading lobes that resemble a star. Each flower produces four cone-shaped, hard and bony seeds, or nutlets—in Greek, litho means stone and sperm means seed.

Puccoon ranges widely in western North America, occupying a number of habitats from sandy plains and gravelly slopes to deep loamy soils of grasslands. It flowers in late spring.

Puccoon and a related species are two of many plants that Plains Indians used widely as a medicine. The roots had a dual function, as a food when cooked and a remedy for respiratory ailments. The common name is of Indian derivation.

Fiddle-neck

Amsinckia species

Species of Amsinckia typify the characteristics of the borage family. The yellow petals are fused into a narrow tube with five perpendicularly spreading lobes. Dense hairs, which cover much of the plant, nearly hide the floral tube. These stiff and bristle-like hairs may penetrate the skin on contact, often causing irritation. A coiled (scorpioid) inflorescence bears the fiddle-neck's trumpet-shaped flowers. Each flower produces four small, hard-shelled, black and shiny nutlets that are reputedly poisonous to cattle. All of several species are annuals with a simple taproot and a branched stem. The leaves are rather narrow and elongate, much longer toward the base of the stem.

Fiddle-neck species are difficult to distinguish. They have similar characteristics and all are weedy plants that thrive on disturbed areas such as roadsides and overgrazed ranges; they cannot compete successfully in unaltered plant communities. Various species grow more or less throughout the sagebrush steppe and flower in early spring.

Sagebrush Stickseed

Hackelia arida

This genus gets its common name from its seeds, or nutlets, covered by minute, branched barbs that catch in the fur (or clothing) of animals, facilitating the seed's dispersal. Sagebrush stickseed typically branches at the base into several stems. The leaves reach several inches long and less than one inch wide. The flowers are white and rather showy. Other characteristics follow basically those of the borage family. This is a common plant in central Washington, extending from the sagebrush steppe into ponderosa pine forests.

Puccoon   *Lithospermum ruderale*

Fiddle-neck   *Amsinckia*

Sagebrush stickseed   *Hackelia arida*

25

BROOMRAPE FAMILY   Orobanchaceae

This small family completely depends upon associated plants for food, nutrients, and water; it's a family of obligate root parasites. Accordingly, the plants lack chlorophyll and are non-photosynthetic. Leaves are reduced and scale-like. The bilaterally symmetrical flowers have adapted for pollination by bees.

Clustered broomrape   *Orobanche fasciculata*

As the name indicates, this plant's rather thick and fleshy stems are clustered, with small, scale-like leaves. Clustered broomrape produces several two- to six-inch flowering stalks, each with a single bilaterally symmetrical flower. Sticky, glandular hairs cover the yellow to purplish stems, leaves, and flowers. The petals are fused into a slightly arched tube with five lobes. The root is fleshy and bulbous.

Because of their parasitic habit, this and other species of broomrape have been able to extend their range beyond that to which they have adapted. For example, although clustered broomrape does not possess adaptations for water preservation, it may rely on a host, such as sagebrush, to provide a constant source.

A common species of moist areas, often growing in seepages, is **naked broomrape** (*Orobanche uniflora*). This broomrape produces non-clustered stems three to six inches tall that bear a single pale blue to purple, bilaterally symmetrical flower. It parasitizes species of the saxifrage family, for example, prairie starflower.

Clustered broomrape   *Orobanche fasciculata*

Purplish naked broomrape *(Orobanche uniflora)*, white-blossomed prairie star flower *(Lithophragma bulbifera)*, and yellow monkey-flower *(Mimulus guttatus)*

BUCKWHEAT FAMILY   Polygonaceae

The buckwheat family contains a few large genera with very different but easily observable characteristics. However, in general the flowers are small and the petals absent or similar in color and size to the sepals. Flower parts appear mostly in multiples of three, and each flower produces a single grain-like seed, or achene.

Desert buckwheat   *Eriogonum* species

As a group, desert buckwheats constitute one of the most important dominants of the sagebrush steppe, behind only grass and sagebrush. Most species prefer gravelly or sandy soils and are often codominants of sagebrush communities; others are dominant members of rocky, or lithosol, communities. All species have adapted well to withstand the summer drought.

With the exception of some mostly small and inconspicuous annuals, the steppe species of *Eriogonum* are long-lived perennials with branched woody stems and densely hairy, basal leaves. The flowers, individually very small, form dense single or multiple umbrella-like clusters, called umbels, at the end of upright, nearly leafless stems. Each small flower has three sepals and three petals, which are usually similar in size, structure and color, and nine stamens. The floral color varies among and within species from white or yellow to pink or reddish. The flowers persist for many days and tend to darken to yellow-red as they age.

The desert buckwheats are attractive plants, especially those with colorful, ball-shaped flower clusters. Most species flower in late spring or early summer, others in early spring, some in late summer. Collectively, they probably provide the single most important nectar source for steppe-inhabiting bees. Seeds provide a major source of food for birds and rodents.

The most important and widespread species of *Eriogonum* is **parsley desert buckwheat (*Eriogonum heracleoides*)**, which grows more or less throughout the steppe. This plant very frequently achieves dominant status in gravelly soils and on rocky ridges. It is shrubby at the base with narrow, densely hairy leaves. The flowering stems usually have a whorl of leaves near mid-length and another whorl below the several flowering stems. Each flowering stem produces one or more ball-like clusters of flowers, usually whitish-yellow becoming reddish in age. The plants bloom in early summer.

A showy species that frequently becomes dominant in the western "half" of the steppe, especially on lithosols, is **round-headed desert buckwheat (*Eriogonum sphaerocephalum*)**, which flowers in early summer. This low, extensively branched shrub produces small (approximately one inch long) woolly leaves (at least on the underside) in whorls at the ends of branches and below the flower clusters. The usually bright yellow flowers are borne in a few to several clusters per stem.

Parsley desert buckwheat   *Eriogonum heracleoides*

Round-headed desert buckwheat   *Eriogonum sphaerocephalum*

A highly variable and attractive species is **oval-leaf desert buckwheat** (*Eriogonum ovalifolium*), which ranges from the sagebrush steppe to alpine ridges. This relatively low plant has many basal, oval woolly leaves and a few to several leafless flowering stems. Each flowering stem bears a dense, ball-shaped cluster of colorful white, reddish, or yellow flowers. This desert buckwheat occupies a wide range of habitats throughout the sagebrush steppe and becomes especially common through eastern Idaho, Wyoming, and the Great Basin. It flowers in early to mid summer.

Another extremely variable and wide ranging species is **umbrella desert buckwheat** (*Eriogonum umbellatum*), which also grows in a multitude of habitats from sagebrush steppe to alpine ridges. The flowers develop in two to six dense clusters and vary in color from white to bright yellow or pink to red. Umbrella desert buckwheat blooms in midsummer or earlier depending on elevation and exposure. The woody stems branch extensively and often form mats. The upright, flowering stems have a whorl of leaves below the flower clusters. This is probably the most common species in the sagebrush "desert" of the Great Basin and adjacent Colorado.

Perhaps the most spectacular of the many species of *Eriogonum* is **northern desert buckwheat** (*Eriogonum compositum*), which ranges from Canada to northeastern California and east into Idaho and Nevada. It produces many clusters, or small umbels, of unusually bright yellow flowers in a flat-topped inflorescence. The plants are very distinctive with their relatively large leaves, several inches long and half as wide. The leaves are triangular or heart-shaped, finely woolly, and all basal.

This desert buckwheat occupies rocky habitats throughout its limited range and flowers in early summer.

One of the most ungainly species is **strict desert buckwheat** (*Eriogonum strictum*). It is an extensively branched shrub, each of the numerous branches bearing a small cluster of whitish to pale yellow or pink flowers. Leaves are all basal, small, oblong, and densely hairy. This variable species is widely distributed in the western "half" of the steppeland, mostly in sandy plains. It flowers in early summer.

Another rather unattractive species is **snow desert buckwheat** (*Eriogonum niveum*). It is conspicuous, however, because it flowers in late summer when other plants of its typical rocky habitat are wasted. Sometimes it grows so abundantly that the landscape appears dusted with snow. It has white or pale pink flowers, only a few per branch. Snow desert buckwheat inhabits the western "half" of the steppe.

Oval-leaf desert buckwheat   *Eriogonum ovalifolium*

Umbrella desert buckwheat   *Eriogonum umbellatum*
Northern desert buckwheat   *Eriogonum compositum*

The desert buckwheats have adapted very well to deal with the drought, heat, and wind of the sagebrush steppe. The leaves protect themselves from the wind by lying on or close to the ground, cushion-like. Also, most species have small leaves with a limited surface area from which water can evaporate. The dense hairiness also protects against water loss by reflecting the radiation of the sun, thus cooling the leaves, and by maintaining a buffer zone of moisture along the leaf surface by reducing air flow. Finally, the plants have extensive and often deep root systems from which they efficiently absorb water. These adaptations prove effective both in the steppes and high mountain ridges where the desert buckwheats are equally at home.

Perhaps the species that best exemplifies the cushion habit is, appropriately, **cushion desert buckwheat (*Eriogonum caespitosum*)**. This plant forms very dense, low mats with many small (less than one inch long) oblong, white-woolly leaves and short, upright flowering stalks. Each stalk bears a single small cluster of yellow flowers that redden with age. The species is widespread from Idaho and Montana east and south through the sagebrush steppe, extending upward along rocky ridges into the alpine zone. It flowers in early summer.

A more attractive cushion species of Washington, Oregon, and Idaho is **thyme desert buckwheat (*Eriogonum thymoides*)**. This compact plant of basaltic soils, or lithosols, has numerous short upright branches each bearing a very dense cluster of yellow, whitish, or pink to rose-red flowers. Long, straight hairs cover the small petals and petal-like sepals. Whitish hairs also densely cover the narrow, less than ½-inch-long, leaves that appear in whorls of several at the base and near mid-length of upright flowering stems. This species flowers in mid spring.

Sand dock   *Rumex venosus*

With its conspicuous reddish sepals and lack of petals, sand dock is both an unusual and attractive member of the buckwheat family. However, it quickly deteriorates into an off-color "eye-sore" as the summer progresses. The plants spread by thick woody rootstalks, called rhizomes, and often form dense populations in sandy habitats. Upright stems are rather succulent and bear several broad and heavily-veined leaves as much as six inches long. Above each leaf is a conspicuous papery sheath, a sheathing stipule. This plant tolerates the nitrogen deficiency so typical of sandy habitats. It also has to deal with being buried by the "shifting, whispering sand" in the dune areas where it most frequently grows—it simply sends up new shoots.

Cushion desert buckwheat *Eriogonum caespitosum*

Thyme desert buckwheat *Eriogonum thymoides*
Sand dock *Rumex venosus*

BUTTERCUP FAMILY   Ranunculaceae

Although this is a diverse family, all species share the characteristics of numerous stamens, three to many pistils, and no fusion of floral parts. Usually the leaves are compound or at least deeply lobed or divided. The majority of the species love moisture but a few are important inhabitants of the steppe.

Sagebrush buttercup   *Ranunculus glaberrimus*

There are many species of buttercups, most requiring moist or wet habitats. The generic name derives in part from the Latin *rana* meaning frog and relates to the aquatic habitat of many or most buttercups. Among those species that have adapted to semi-arid conditions, the sagebrush buttercup is the showiest and probably the most widespread. This very early-flowering plant favors the less dry sites and frequently grows under large shrubs such as sagebrush or bitterbrush (*Purshia tridentata*). Sagebrush buttercup is a small, branched, usually prostrate herb with dark green, rather fleshy, shallowly lobed leaves, and clustered fleshy roots. The attractive flowers usually exceed one inch in diameter with five (occasionally four, six, or seven) very bright, waxy-shiny, yellow petals, smaller yellowish-purplish sepals, and numerous stamens and pistils.

Sagebrush buttercup lives more or less throughout the high plains of the sagebrush steppe and extends into ponderosa pine forests and piñon-juniper woodlands.

Vase flower   *Clematis hirsutissima*

Vase flower is a distinctive and attractive plant with fern-like leaves and unusual flowers. The stems, twelve to eighteen inches tall, bear several large, extensively-divided leaves. The solitary flowers, approximately one inch long, nod as inverted vases at the stem tips. As is typical in species of *Clematis*, the flowers lack petals but the showy sepals resemble petals. In this species the sepals are thick and leathery (yielding the common name, leather flower) and have the unusual color of brownish-purple. Each flower has several woolly ovaries, which develop long, feathery styles as they mature into hard, single-seeded fruits called achenes. The style remains attached to the achene and aids in its dispersal by the wind. Dense hair covers the entire plant.

Vase flower is equally at home in the high plains and in the mountains. It inhabits all but the southernmost extent of the steppeland. Some Plains Indians considered this plant to have healing powers.

34

Sagebrush buttercup *Ranunculus glaberrimus*

Vase flower (flower)
Clematis hirsutissima

Vase flower (fruits)
Clematis hirsutissima

Larkspur   *Delphinium* species

All larkspurs have bilaterally symmetrical flowers with numerous stamens. The upper sepal extends into a rather long, nectar-bearing spur. The
two lower petals are much broader than the upper two, which are white with
purple nectar guides that direct bumblebees to the nectar source. Each flower
produces three to five, many-seeded, pod-like fruits called follicles. The leaves
are palmately lobed or divided.

Although the larkspurs have beautiful, ornate flowers, they are not
particularly welcome on rangeland. All species produce alkaloids that are
toxic to livestock; death by larkspur poisoning is not uncommon.

The most widespread and variable species of larkspur is **common larkspur** *(Delphinium nuttallianum)*, distributed from moist mountain meadows and open forests to dry sandy sagebrush plains. With the exception of
some of the drier sites, it grows essentially throughout the steppe. The
variation is expressed in many ways: the normally blue to purple sepals vary
to nearly pure white; the roots may be rather thin and woody, thick and fleshy,
or intermediate; the upper part of the stem and the flowers are usually hairy,
the nature of which varies from sparse to dense and matted or even glandular-
sticky.

Perhaps the showiest of the larkspurs is **western larkspur** *(Delphinium
bicolor)*, a common species of Idaho, Wyoming, and Montana. This low-
growing plant produces only a few large flowers per stem. It extends well up
into the mountains on open ridges.

Larkspurs are of two basic types: the short-stemmed, few-flowered forms
with showy flowers, such as the two species noted above, and the tall and
robust, many-flowered forms. The former group consists primarily of steppe
and prairie species; the robust species grow mostly in forests but inhabit the
more moist regions of the sagebrush steppe. The most widespread of the tall
species is **showy larkspur** *(Delphinium occidentale)*. This plant has few
to several, branched stems as much as six feet tall. The flowers, numerous and
small, form narrow and elongate racemes at the ends of branches. Floral color
varies from dark blue to white. The large leaves are palmately divided. This
is probably the most poisonous of the many larkspurs of the sagebrush steppe.
It inhabits the plains and open forests of the Rocky Mountain region.

Common larkspur
Delphinium nuttallianum

Western larkspur
Delphinium occidentale

Showy larkspur *Delphinium bicolor*

CACTUS FAMILY Cactaceae

The cactus family is very well adapted to dry climates. The leaves have modified into spines, greatly reducing water loss, and the succulent stems store an abundance of water. The shallow roots branch extensively, enabling the plants to absorb water quickly after storms. The flowers are generally large and showy with several petals and numerous stamens. The ovary is inferior, that is, the petals and other flower parts develop on rather than below the ovary. The fruit is fleshy at maturity.

Few species of cacti inhabit the sagebrush steppe, but they become increasingly more numerous toward the south where they often become the dominant members of desert communities.

Prickly pear cactus *Opuntia polyacantha*

Few flowers are as attractive as those of cacti in general and prickly pear in particular. The flowers are usually lemon-yellow or peach-color (becoming pink or orange with age) but may be brilliant red, as they frequently are in Nevada and southern Idaho. These multi-petaled flowers appear as outgrowths from terminal, somewhat flattened, pear-shaped stem segments, which are well armed with long, needle-sharp spines. (*Polyacantha* means "many spines.")

Widespread and variable in habit, prickly pear grows most frequently in sandy soils with individual plants rather widely scattered. However, overgrazing enhances the prickly pears' ability to spread through the elimination of competitors, the creation of new, disturbed habitats, and the physical dispersal of stem segments, each of which can develop into a new plant.

Hedgehog cactus *Pediocactus simpsonii*

The round or barrel-shaped hedgehog cactus is somewhat of an oddity in the sagebrush steppe and would seem to be more at home in the deserts of the Southwest. This small cactus, seldom over eight inches tall, often grows in small clumps. The round stems are covered with vertical rows of swollen areas, called tubercles, each of which produces several spreading, rigid, needle-sharp spines. The showy rose to purple or yellowish flowers bloom without stalks at the top of the cactus. Each flower is one to one-and-a-half inches wide with numerous petals and stamens.

Hedgehog cactus is much less common than the prickly pear and tends to be restricted to rocky hillsides and plains, usually in lithosol areas. Unfortunately, collectors frequently dig up the plants, though they seldom survive under cultivation. In some areas where this cactus was once common it is now rare. Hedgehog cactus does have a wide range, however, including a large part of the sagebrush steppe.

Yellow prickly pear cactus   *Opuntia polyacantha*

Red prickly pear cactus   *Opuntia polyacantha*

Hedgehog cactus   *Pediocactus simpsonii*

CAPER FAMILY   Capparidaceae

Yellow bee plant   *Cleome lutea*

The flowers of the caper family closely resemble those of mustards with four sepals, four petals, six stamens, and a narrow pod-like fruit. They are distinct from those of mustards, however, in that the stamens extend well beyond the petals, giving the inflorescence a brush-like appearance.

A family rather closely related to the caper family is the Fumitory family. The common representative of the fumitory family in the sagebrush steppe is **Golden corydalis (*Corydalis aurea*)**. It also produces four petals, six stamens, and a pod-like fruit, but differs conspicuously from capers in having bilaterally symmetrical flowers with a pouch-like projection or spur at the base of the petals. The leaves are divided and parsley-like. This widespread species of the sagebrush steppe frequently grows along roadsides in gravely soils.

Yellow bee plant   *Cleome lutea*

The yellow bee plant combines a number of features that make it both unusual and very attractive. Most noticeable are its bright, golden-yellow flowers at the end of the stems, densely crowded into a showy cluster that elongates as the plant matures. Each flower has four narrow sepals, four yellow petals, and six stamens that are considerably longer than the petals and contribute to the general showiness of the flower cluster. The pod-like fruits, shaped by the large seeds they contain, develop first at the base of the flower cluster and hang gracefully on narrow stalks, called pedicels.

These erect annuals have a single, often branched stem reaching as much as three feet tall. The attractive leaves are palmately compound, or lupine-like, with five elliptical leaflets spreading as "fingers" from a central point. Upper stem leaves are small and cluster bract-like around the base of the flower.

The yellow bee plant is very common regionally in sandy plains of the western deserts and steppes and a conspicuous dominant in some areas of the Great Basin, especially in Utah and adjacent Colorado. It flowers over a period of several weeks beginning in late spring.

Golden bee plant   *Cleome platycarpa*

This species differs from the yellow bee plant in having clover-like, (trifoliate) leaves and flattened pods (*platycarpa* means flat fruits). The habitat and distribution of the two species are similar.

Yellow bee plant *Cleome lutea*   **Golden bee plant** *Cleome platycarpa*

Golden corydalis *Corydalis aurea*

CURRANT FAMILY   Grossulariaceae

The small currant family comprises a single genus that includes the currants and gooseberries. All species are medium-sized shrubs with alternate, palmately lobed or compound leaves. Several of the species sport thorns or prickles. The sepals, fused into a tube or a "saucer," are larger and more conspicuously colored than the petals. The ovary is inferior and matures into a many-seeded berry. Most species grow in meadows or along streams. However, the two species described below extend into steppe communities.

Squaw currant   *Ribes cereum*

Squaw currant is a medium-sized shrub with brownish stems and palmately-lobed, gray-green leaves. The flowers form small clusters at the end of short stalks along the branches. The greenish-white to pinkish sepals are fused into a tube with five spreading lobes. The petals are small, fan-shaped, and inconspicuous. Although the flowers are not showy, the fruit is, becoming orange-red when ripe. The fruit, though not particularly palatable, may result in a burning sensation in the throat if eaten in a sufficiently large quantity. Glandular, often-sticky hairs on the younger branches, leaf stalks, flowers, and fruits contribute to the rather strong, unpleasant odor of the plants, somewhat resembling carrion. Nevertheless, the plants provide an important food source for deer.

Squaw currant is a common shrub on coarse talus slopes, particularly in the higher altitudes and latitudes of the sagebrush steppe, extending upward into open forests and ridges. It grows in suitable habitats more or less throughout the steppeland.

Another species of wild currant that occasionally inhabits the steppeland is **golden currant (*Ribes aureum*)**, an attractive shrub with golden-yellow flowers. The tasty orangish fruit makes excellent jelly. The shrub's three-lobed leaves are bright green and somewhat leathery. Golden currant grows mainly along the gravel banks and flood plains of streams and rivers.

Squaw currant *Ribes cereum*

Flowering golden currant *Ribes aureum*

Golden currant (*Ribes aureum)* bearing fruit

EPHEDRA FAMILY   Ephedraceae

Species of Ephedra are unusual in several aspects. They lack flowers and the seeds develop in small cone-like structures at the junctures of jointed stems. The leaves are reduced and appear as small bracts or scales, also at stem joints. The stems are green and photosynthetic with numerous stiff, upright, broom-like branches. The various ephedras are widely distributed in the arid southwest, particularly in desert mountains of California, Nevada, and Utah, extending southward into Mexico.

Green ephedra (*Ephedra viridis*) is prevalent along the transitional zone between piñon-juniper woodlands and drier communities. In central Nevada its distribution widely overlaps with sagebrush, although it is more common farther south in the Mojave Desert. The antidepressant and anticongestive drug ephedrine occurs naturally as an alkaloid in Ephedra. The stems have historically been dried for use as a slightly pungent tea, yielding the frequently applied common names of Mexican and Mormon tea.

EVENING PRIMROSE FAMILY   Onagraceae

The floral "formula" identifies this family: four sepals, four petals, eight stamens (usually), and a four-chambered, inferior ovary. The fruit matures into an elongate, many-seeded capsule.

Clarkia   *Clarkia pulchella*

Clarkia flowers are highly attractive with their distinctive one-inch-long, pink-lavender to rose-purple, or rarely white, petals with a broad, three-lobed tip and a very narrow minutely toothed base. Typical of the family, all floral parts come in sets of four, including an elongate, conspicuous four-lobed style. This locally common, widely distributed annual grows in dry, sandy soils in open forests and steppelands where it is often associated with sagebrush. It extends from Washington and Oregon through Idaho. The genus was named in honor of Captain William Clark of the Lewis and Clark Expedition. The species name, *pulchella*, means beautiful and is appropriately applied.

Green ephedra   *Ephedra viridis*

Clarkia   *Clarkia pulchella*

Clarkia   *Clarkia pulchella*

Evening primrose   *Oenothera* species

This genus comprises a number of attractive, fragrant and often nocturnal desert and/or steppe species. As a group they are recognizable by a combination of floral parts in multiples of four plus the long, narrow floral tube arising from the ovary. The long tube is an evolutionary adaptation for pollination by long-tongued hawk moths. Most species are low, essentially stemless plants with many basal rosette leaves.

The most widespread and attractive evening primrose is **desert evening primrose (*Oenothera caespitosa*)** with its large and showy white flowers that turn pink with age, both colors frequently occurring simultaneously on a plant. The petals reach as much as two inches long and wide with a deeply notched tip making them heart-shaped. The plants lack stems so the flowers and elongate leaves are borne on the rootcrown. This species grows most frequently on talus slopes or in sandy plains throughout western North America.

A very similar but short-stemmed, somewhat smaller-flowered plant is *Oenothera deltoides*. This species has a southerly distribution, growing more frequently in the Mojave Desert than in the sagebrush steppe.

White-stemmed evening primrose (*Oenothera pallida*) is a common species of partially stabilized sand dunes and other sandy areas west of the Continental Divide. Its stems reach up to eighteen inches tall with many narrow and elongate, often toothed leaves. The white flowers arise from the axis of the upper leaves and turn pink with age. The petals are approximately one inch long.

A species from east of the Continental Divide that somewhat resembles the white-stemmed evening primrose in form and size is *Oenothera trichocalyx*. This widespread species grows on gravelly hillsides and in sandy plains of Wyoming, Colorado, and Utah.

Two attractive yellow-flowered evening primroses are **tansy-leaved evening primrose (*Oenothera tanecetifolia*)** and *Oenothera brachycarpa*. The latter is a large-flowered, stemless species of southerly distribution, reaching the sagebrush steppe in Nevada. Its bright yellow petals turn reddish with age. Tansy-leaved evening primrose grows in heavy loam or clay soils of lowland, moist areas west of the Continental Divide. It is a low, stemless plant with deeply lobed or divided leaves and brilliant yellow flowers. The petals are somewhat less than one inch long.

Several additional species of evening primrose inhabit the sagebrush steppe, most annuals with small yellow or white flowers. Some are stemless, low plants, others have leafy stems.

Desert evening primrose *Oenothera caespitosa*

White-stemmed evening primrose *Oenothera pallida*

Tansy-leaved evening primrose *Oenothera tanecetifolia*

FIGWORT FAMILY   Scrophulariaceae

One of the largest families, the figworts include many of the most beautiful wildflowers of the sagebrush steppe. The family varies widely to include shrubs and herbs; the leaves may be alternate or opposite, compound or simple. The flowers also vary in shape but all are bilaterally symmetrical and have pod-like fruits, usually with numerous small seeds. The typical figwort flower typifies a bumblebee pollination design: unique, recognizable shapes and color patterns; nectar concealed within a tube; bilateral symmetry with a landing pad for the bee; nectar guides that promote repeated floral entry by the bee; and stamens and stigma precisely positioned to contact the bee in just the right spot for efficient pollination.

Monkey-flower   *Mimulus* species

The name *Mimulus* comes from the Latin *mimus* meaning mimic, especially mimic actor. Presumably the flowers of *Mimulus*, with their "grinning face," mimic monkeys. A number of small annual species of monkey flower, including both yellow- and red-flowered forms, inhabit the steppes and deserts of North America. All produce showy, bilaterally symmetrical flowers with a basal tube and spreading petal lobes. The lower three lobes form a well-marked landing platform with longitudinal, hairy ridges. The sepals fuse into a tube with pointed lobes.

The two most common red-flowered species are **dwarf purple monkey-flower** (*Mimulus nanus*), mostly from the eastern "half" of sagebrush country, and **cusick's monkey-flower** (*Mimulus cusickii*), from the western "half" of the steppe. Both are small annuals. The flowers of the dwarf purple monkey-flower are deep magenta with dark red and yellow markings in the throat of the tube. Cusick's monkey-flower produces lighter flowers with broad yellow bands in the throat. Both species occupy dry, sandy or gravelly sites and flower in early summer. Where they form very dense populations, both species, especially dwarf purple monkey-flower, provide spectacular displays of color.

Yellow monkey flower   *Mimulus guttatus*

The yellow monkey flower shows extreme variation, both in size and geographical distribution. It grows most frequently in the mud and gravel of slow-moving, small streams. Here it is a tall, showy perennial, often associated with watercress. It also occasionally inhabits seepage areas throughout the sagebrush steppe. In this habitat it exists mostly as a small, few-flowered annual, an adaptation that enables the plants to complete their life cycle very quickly. The population survives in the form of seeds during dry periods when the seepage stops. In the spring the dense population offers a spectacular display of brilliant yellow flowers with red splotches marking the landing platform (hence, the name "guttatus" meaning spotted).

Dwarf purple monkey-flower *Mimulus nanus*

Cusick's monkey flower *Minulus cusickii*

Yellow monkey-flower *Mimulus guttatus*

Penstemon or beardtongue   *Penstemon* species

The various species of penstemon include some of the most attractive plants of the sagebrush steppe. The flowers, both colorful and attractively sculptured, vary in color from white to yellowish or pale lavender to deep blue or purple. The flower has five stamens (penta-stamen), only four of which produce pollen. The fifth, sterile stamen underwent various modifications in the process of evolution. Frequently it is covered with golden hair that gives it the fancied appearance of a bearded tongue within the throat of the floral tube, yielding the common name of beardtongue. Plants usually have several rather coarse, erect stems with opposite, sometimes toothed or lobed leaves. The basal leaves are usually elliptical and have stalks called petioles; the upper leaves are often lance-shaped, lack petioles, and become progressively smaller and more bract-like toward the stem tip. The flowers form whorls of a few to several in the axils of the upper leaves. The fruit, a hard, somewhat woody capsule, splits open at maturity releasing the numerous small seeds.

The tall, blue-flowered penstemons include some of the most common species in the steppe. These plants have one to several stems, up to three feet tall, arising from the rootcrown. The bright blue flowers are up to two inches long and unusually attractive. A common representative of this group is **showy penstemon (*Penstemon speciosus*)**. It has elongate, blue-green, leathery leaves, the basal ones long-stalked, the stem leaves lacking stalks. It grows most commonly in Washington, Oregon, California, Nevada, and southwestern Idaho. Two very similar tall, blue-flowered penstemons are **blue penstemon (*Penstemon cyaneus*)**, a conspicuous plant in the sandy sagebrush plains of eastern Idaho and adjacent Utah, Wyoming, and Montana, and **mountain penstemon (*Penstemon alpinus*)**, occurring in the high plains and mountains of the Great Basin and adjacent Colorado.

A very common penstemon of sandy plains and partially stabilized dunes in the steppes of northern Nevada and adjacent California, Oregon, Washington, and southwestern Idaho is **sand penstemon (*P. acuminatus*)**. This medium-sized plant (1/2 to two feet tall) produces thick and leathery, blue-green, mostly basal leaves. Its bright blue to blue-purple flowers, less than one inch long, cluster in several whorls near the stem tip. The entire plant is often sticky, or glutinous.

Lowly penstemon (*Penstemon humilus*) is a somewhat similar species but smaller in all aspects, especially the flowers. The stems are also more strictly erect and the flowers have a very narrow tube. This species commonly grows west of the Continental Divide, extending from the dry steppe up to open rocky ridges at high elevations.

Showy penstemon   *Penstemon speciosus*   Lowly penstemon   *Penstemon humilus*

Sand penstemon   *Penstemon acuminatus*

Penstemon constitues a large and taxonomically difficult genus. The characteristics of the species are similar, and apparently some species hybridize when their ranges overlap. Still, a great deal of variation exists within the genus. The species considered here represent the range of variation and geographic distribution of species that grow in the sagebrush steppe. The species occupy a wide variety of habitats, from lithosols or sand dunes to deep loamy soils.

A frequent plant of dry, rocky (lithosol and talus) habitats more or less throughout the sagebrush steppe is **scorched penstemon (*Penstemon deustus*)**. It is especially common in the basaltic areas of southeastern Idaho. This rather low, many-stemmed plant produces sharply and deeply toothed leaves. The white flowers, approximately one half inch long, usually have lavender stripes that serve as nectar guides extending from the mouth of the tube down into the throat.

Two similar species in terms of size, growth form, and floral characteristics are **rock penstemon (*Penstemon gairdneri*)** and larchleaf penstemon (*Penstemon laricifolius*). Both are low, many-stemmed plants with narrow leaves and pale lavender, one-half- to three-quarter-inch-long flowers. Both also grow in dry, rocky (lithosol) sites: rock penstemon in Washington, Oregon, and adjacent Idaho and larchleaf penstemon in the eastern "half" of the steppeland. In dense populations they offer beautiful displays of color in their respective locations.

Two attractive, small-flowered species of rocky habitats are **Wilcox's penstemon (*Penstemon wilcoxii*)** and Chelan penstemon (*Penstemon pruinosus*). Both produce dark blue or blue-lavender flowers approximately one half inch long (or smaller in the latter species). The two species are many-stemmed plants with toothed leaves and sticky hair, especially on and around the flowers. Wilcox's penstemon inhabits the high steppes and mountains west of the Continental Divide; Chelan penstemon is locally common in the rainshadow of the Cascade Range.

Certainly one of the most spectacular species of Penstemon, **prairie penstemon (*Penstemon cobaea*)**, barely reaches into the sagebrush steppe of Utah and Colorado from the prairies to the east. This very tall plant, up to four feet with few stems, produces large, two- to three-inch-long flowers with an inflated throat. The flowers are pale lavender with darker stripes that serve as nectar guides. Stiff golden hairs densely cover the sterile stamen, blocking the entrance to the floral tube and preserving the nectar for bumblebees. The hairy stamen also elevates the rear end of the bee ensuring that the bee contacts the stamens and stigma at the top of the tube.

Scorched penstemon *Penstemon deustus*

Rock penstemon *Penstemon gairdneri*

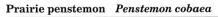

Wilcox's penstemon *Penstemon wilcoxii*

Prairie penstemon *Penstemon cobaea*

As noted in the discussions above, the typical penstemon flower is structured to be pollinated by bees, especially bumblebees. The petals fuse into a nectar-containing tube with five lobes, two projecting upward, the other three usually extending downward and outward to provide a landing platform for foraging bees. In most species the landing platform displays recognizable markings—sometimes nectar guides, often glistening hairs. The fertile stamens are fused in precise position at the top of the floral tube. The stigma is also located at the top of the "mouth." The bee alights on the landing pad and moves forward into the tube, first touching the stigma and depositing pollen from a previous flower visited, then picking up additional pollen that it will carry to the next flower. The bee receives its reward in nectar that she collects at the base of the floral tube. Occasionally, she also gathers pollen to take back to the hive.

Some penstemons lack the well-differentiated landing platforms and are pollinated by long-tongued animals other than bees. Red-flowered penstemons, adapted for pollination by hummingbirds, provide the most conspicuous examples. One such species is **firecracker penstemon (*Penstemon eatonii*)** with brilliant, crimson flowers forming long, narrow tubes. This spectacular species lives throughout the high plains, open forests, and mountain ridges of central Nevada, Utah, and the southern Rockies. It most frequently grows on talus slopes.

Another red-flowered species, **cutleaf penstemon (*Penstemon richardsonii*)** derives its name from its deeply divided leaves. However, the flowers are typical of penstemons with a landing pad and a conspicuously inflated throat with nectar guides. This tall (up to three feet) weak-stemmed plant has only limited distribution, growing along talus slopes in central Washington and Oregon.

A species with flowers almost intermediate in shape and color between bee and hummingbird types is **whipple's penstemon (*Penstemon whippleanus*)**. This attractive plant usually has reddish-purple, inch-long, sticky-hairy flowers with the lower lip conspicuously longer than the upper. The clustered stems reach up to two feet tall. The basal leaves are elliptical and long-stalked; the stem leaves are reduced in size and non-stalked. This penstemon grows from Montana south through the southern Rockies. It extends upward from the steppelands into open forests and onto ridges at high elevations.

Firecracker penstemon *Penstemon eatonii*

Cutleaf penstemon *Penstemon richardsonii*

Whipple's penstemon *Penstemon whippleanus*

Indian paintbrush   *Castilleja* species

Few inhabitants of the sagebrush steppe prove as striking as the Indian paintbrushes. Although the flowers are rather small and non-showy, they bloom amid many colorful bract-like leaves that help attract pollinators, especially hummingbirds. The petals fuse into a narrow, elongate, greenish-red tube that may or may not extend beyond the bracts. A slit opens the upper half of the floral tube on the outer side, enabling access to the nectar rewards by a hummingbird or long-tongued insect. The stamens and style project at the tip of the tube. The sepals are partially fused and colored similarly to the bracts. Most paintbrushes are perennials with woody, well-branched root systems. Stiff hairs cover most plants.

Several species of paintbrush are native to the sagebrush steppe, many very similar and difficult to distinguish. Adding to this difficulty is the large amount of variation of some recognized species, especially in floral and bract color. Also, typical of most large genera, related species commonly hybridize when ranges overlap, resulting in additional complications.

Perhaps the most widespread and variable species is **desert paintbrush** (*Castilleja chromosa*), with flower clusters varying in color from brilliant crimson to shades of red, orange, or yellow, even within a single population. The lower leaves are long and narrow and undivided; the upper leaves and the bracts are divided into three to five narrow segments. This species resembles and hybridizes with linear-leafed paintbrush (*Castilleja linariaefolia*), a rather spectacular species honored as the state flower of Wyoming. Desert paintbrush is more widely distributed, however, very commonly inhabiting the southern part of the Great Basin and the eastern "half" of the sagebrush steppe.

A second species that closely resembles desert paintbrush is **narrow-leaf paintbrush** (*Castilleja angustifolia*). Its inflorescence also varies in color, but typically the bracts and sepals take on a unique and beautiful, purplish-rose coloration, distinguishing the plant from other species. The lower leaves are long, narrow, and undivided, and the upper leaves and bracts divide into three to five segments. Short, straight hairs cover the leaves and stems. Narrow-leaf paintbrush grows most commonly in Idaho, Montana, and Wyoming, usually in association with sagebrush.

Desert paintbrush (yellow)
Castilleja chromosa

Narrow-leaf paintbrush
Castilleja angustifolia

Desert paintbrush (red) *Castilleja chromosa*

Paintbrushes have adapted to parasitize the roots of associated plants, especially sagebrush. From the host plant, the paintbrush derives both water and organic materials, a source of energy. Through this parasitic association, the paintbrush increases its tolerance to dry conditions and expands its geographical range. However, the paintbrushes are facultative parasites— they can survive in the absence of a host but lose the benefits noted above. Unlike penstemons, which grow mostly in rocky habitats, paintbrushes usually prefer the deeper, sandy soils. This undoubtedly relates to the similar requirements of host plants such as sagebrush.

Many of the paintbrushes have a broad elevational range, from dry steppes to high mountain ridges. One of our most attractive such species is **mountain paint-brush** (*Castilleja applegatei*), with crimson or bright red inflorescences. The leaves are usually non-divided toward the base of the stem and divided above, as are the bracts. The leaves are also characteristically wavy along the margins and frequently sticky-hairy. This species most commonly inhabits the high plains of eastern Oregon, southern Idaho, Nevada, Utah, and Wyoming.

Perhaps our least attractive species is **Thompson's paintbrush** (*Castilleja thompsonii*), a non-colorful plant with greenish-yellow bracts. It is the most widespread species in the Washington steppe. The stems cluster and usually reach less than one foot tall. The lower leaves are very narrow, or linear, and non-divided, the upper divided into linear segments. Short, white hairs cover the stems and leaves. Contrary to the general rule, Thompson's paintbrush grows primarily on lithosols, perhaps because its principle host is stiff sagebrush (*Artemisia rigida*), a lithosol species.

The only sagebrush paintbrush that is not a perennial herb is **annual paintbrush** (*Castilleja exilis*), obviously an annual. This species is unusual in other aspects as well. The inflorescence bracts are much longer than the flowers, are very narrow and undivided (as are the leaves), and are stiffly erect. The flowers themselves are greenish-yellow; the bracts crimson. Annual paintbrush grows more or less throughout the sagebrush steppe but seldom becomes abundant. It favors somewhat alkaline soils.

Mountain paintbrush *Castilleja applegatei*

Annual paintbrush
Castilleja exilis

Thompson's paintbrush
Castilleja thompsonii

59

Great Plains paintbrush (*Castilleja sessiliflora*) is one of the most distinctive of the numerous species of Castilleja occupying the sagebrush steppe. The fused petals form a very long tube that fancifully resembles a snake reared up in a defensive position, with an arched "neck" and open mouth. The sepals are shorter than the petal tube and have narrow lobes. The inflorescence bracts are short and relatively inconspicuous. The inflorescence (including the bracts and flowers) displays a mixture of shades of green, yellow and pink. A hawk moth, with a tongue long enough to reach to the base of the floral tube, principally pollinates this plant. As the common name suggests, this species grows largely in the Great Plains east of the Rocky Mountains. It reaches into the sagebrush steppe only in Montana, Wyoming, Utah, and Colorado.

Owl-clover   *Orthocarpus* species

Upon casual observation, species of *Orthocarpus* resemble the closely related Indian paintbrushes. Both have rather inconspicuous tubular flowers partially hidden among often colorful, bract-like leaves. However, paintbrushes usually are more colorful and are mostly perennials, with thick, woody roots. Owl-covers are all small annuals less than twelve inches tall. Also in *Orthocarpus*, the fused petals form a two-lipped tube: the hood-like upper lip often hooks forward; the lower lip is usually inflated, with three sacs and three minute, tooth-like projections. Like other annuals, owl-clovers flower early and complete their life cycle before the drought sets in.

A number of species of owl-clover inhabit the sagebrush steppe, particularly the western "half." All prefer somewhat sandy sites and usually grow in association with sagebrush. The most attractive species is **thin-leaved owl-clover** (*Orthocarpus tenuifolius*), with conspicuous pink-purple, petal-like bracts and yellow flowers. The leaves are divided into three to five very narrow segments. This species grows in the rain shadow of the Cascade Range, extending east into Idaho and Montana.

The most widespread species of owl-clover are the golden-yellow-flowered *Orthocarpus luteus* and the white-flowered *Orthocarpus hispidus*.

A rather attractive species of more limited distribution, growing only in the rain shadow of the Cascades in Washington and southern British Columbia, is **Grand Coulee owl-clover** (*Orthocarpus barbatus*). This plant produces bright yellow flowers and greenish-yellow bracts. The leaves and bracts are divided into long, narrow segments.

Great Plains paintbrush *Castilleja sessiliflora*

Thin-leaved owl-clover
Orthocarpus tenuifolius

Grand Coulee owl-clover
Orthocarpus barbatus

61

FLAX FAMILY   Linaceae

This is a small family with a single genus (*Linum*). The herbaceous plants produce attractive flowers with floral parts in multiples of five.

Wild flax   *Linum perenne*

Flax is well marked and easily distinguished from all other inhabitants of the sagebrush steppe. This rather tall plant (up to three feet) has several unbranched stems arising from a somewhat woody rootcrown. The leaves are numerous, narrow, and about one inch long. The most conspicuous aspect of flax is its showy sky-blue flowers, one to two inches across with darker veins, borne near the tip of the thin, flexuous stems. The attractive petals, five per flower, soon fall off if the stems break; therefore the flowers cannot be picked for bouquets.

Flax is an extremely widely distributed plant, occupying suitable habitats throughout the sagebrush steppe. Most frequently it grows in sandy plains, commonly associated with sagebrush or rabbitbrush (*Chrysothamnus*). However, it may extend well up into the mountains where it grows on non-forested gravelly ridges, again associated with sagebrush, or in open savanna-like communities, such as piñon-juniper woodlands or ponderosa pine forests.

Like the cultivated form, flax produces tough fibrous stems that can be used for making cordage. Indians had many uses for flax twine, including fishing lines and net construction.

GERANIUM FAMILY   Geraniaceae

Probably the most outstanding characteristic of the genus, *Geranium* (and the entire geranium family) is the unique shape of the mature fruit. Each flower produces a five-lobed ovary with a long, thick style. As the ovary/fruit matures, the style elongates resembling the bill of a crane, the ovary being the head. Because of this resemblance, the family is often called the crane's-bill family (in Greek, *geranos* means crane). Ultimately, the five lobes separate, each carrying a single seed. Most species bear showy flowers with five large, white to purple petals. The leaves are palmately divided into sharply toothed segments.

Two species of wild geranium (*Geranium*) are distributed over much of western North America: white geranium (*Geranium richardsonii*), with white or pale pink flowers, and **sticky geranium (*Geranium viscosissimum*)**, with deep pink to purple flowers. Glandular, sticky hairs cover both species and are responsible for the typical odor. Sticky geranium is the most attractive and widespread. It grows about two feet tall and branches into many leafy stems, each with several attractive, saucer-shaped flowers. The petals are about one half inch long. Both wild geraniums grow most frequently in and around the upper limits of the sagebrush steppe, becoming especially common in aspen groves. Wild geraniums are favorite forage plants for several animals, especially elk and moose, which prefer the flowers.

Wild flax
Linum perenne

Sticky geranium
Geranium viscosissimum

Sticky geranium   *Geranium viscosissimum*

GOOSEFOOT FAMILY   Chenopodiaceae

If colorful flowers were the only criterion for inclusion in this book, the goosefoot family would not be represented. Flowers are small and inconspicuous, tightly clustered, and often unisexual—typical characteristics of wind-pollinated flowers. In other respects the family varies widely, ranging from small annuals to rather large, often spiny, shrubs. Perhaps the most outstanding adaptation of most species is their ability to tolerate, or even require, alkaline soils. Species are often succulent. The goosefoot family is very well represented in the southwest deserts of North America where some species are frequently major dominants. Species of *Atriplex* often grow in association with sagebrush in the Great Basin. Some species become common weeds along roadsides.

Hopsage   *Atriplex spinosa*

Hopsage is a medium-sized, unisexual shrub with a profile similar to that of sagebrush. The spiny, grayish stems bear many elliptical leaves, about one inch long. The flowers are small and inconspicuous, little more than stamens in male plants or pistils in female plants. However, as the seeds of the female plants mature, each becomes enclosed by two enlarged bracts which vary in color from whitish or greenish to shades of red, making the female plants rather attractive.

Hopsage grows in a wide variety of habitats from talus slopes to alkaline flats, from dry sagebrush plains to the Mojave Desert. It flowers in early spring, but the fruits with their showy bracts do not achieve full color until early summer.

This species has traditionally been placed in the genus *Grayia*, which was named in honor of Dr. Asa Gray, one of the most renowned North American botanists. His *Flora of North America* still ranks high among taxonomic treatments. He was also a consultant to Sir Charles Darwin and a great 19th Century teacher. More recent botanists (for example, Hitchcock in his most recent flora) argue that the distinction between Grayia and Atriplex is not sufficient to put hopsage in a separate genus.

Winterfat   *Eurotia lanata*

Winterfat is an interesting though not particularly attractive shrub with many low, erect branches covered by white woolly or felt-like hairs. The generic name comes from the Greek *euro*, which means mold and refers to the "moldy," whitish coloration of the plants. *Lanata* is of Latin derivation and means wool. The small flowers appear as balls of cotton where the short, narrow leaves meet the stem.

Winter fat grows in dry, salty or alkaline flats in the deserts and steppes of western North America. Usually it grows in association with other salt-tolerant plants (halophytes) but often forms pure stands distinguished by the low stature and whitish color of the plants. It is a highly desirable browse plant and has been used by sheep herders as winter feed for their herds; hence the common name.

Hopsage community *Atriplex spinosa*

Hopsage *Atriplex spinosa*

Winterfat *Eurotia lanata*

Greasewood   *Sarcobatus vermiculatus*

Greasewood, a white-barked shrub that may grow to be several feet tall, is clearly distinguished from sagebrush and most other steppe shrubs by its bright green, rather than grayish, foliage. The numerous small, linear leaves are succulent (in Greek, *sarco* means fleshy) and roundish to triangular in cross section. The many spiny branches earn it the Greek suffix *batus*, which means bramble. The inconspicuous flowers are unisexual. The male flowers form small cone-shaped structures at the ends of small branches, and the female flowers develop where the leaves meet the stem below the "cone."

Greasewood grows in alkaline flats and playas. It can tolerate excessive soil salts which would draw the water out of less well adapted plants. Its ability to absorb and retain water in salty soils is dependent upon the accumulation of sodium salts in the leaf and root tissue. These salts are readily detectable in the taste of the fleshy leaves.

Greasewood often forms extensive populations in salt flats, with the exclusion of almost all other vegetation. Usually it inhabits areas where abundant ground water is available to its deeply penetrating root system. The plant is distributed throughout the sagebrush steppe and is an excellent indicator of alkaline soils.

Russian thistle, tumbleweed   *Salsola kali*

Although Russian thistle was introduced from Eurasia, it has now established itself throughout the steppeland. It owes its distribution efficiency to its annual habit and circular growth form. When the plants die in the autumn, they break away from their roots and tumble freely in the wind, often for many miles, scattering seeds as they go. Fortunately, Russian thistle is not an aggressive competitor; thus, it cannot replace native species. Rather, it grows along roadsides, fence lines, wheat field margins, overgrazed pastures, and other areas where the steppe communities have been disrupted. This remarkable plant does all its growing during late summer when the water supply has essentially been depleted. It "avoids" the drought by combining efficiency in water retention, storage, and absorption.

Russian thistle is truly a noxious weed, both because of its distributional pattern and its general spininess. This extensively branched herbaceous plant produces numerous narrow, needle-like, fleshy leaves and bracts, all rigid and spine-tipped. The stems and branches vary in color from green to red, often with darker stripes. The small and inconspicuous flowers appear at the base of leaves and bracts. The petals (or sepals) look papery and are generally the same color as the stems. The generic name is derived from the Latin *salsus* meaning salty.

Greasewood community near Elko, Nevada

Greasewood *Sarcobatus vermiculatus*
Russian thistle *Salsola kali*

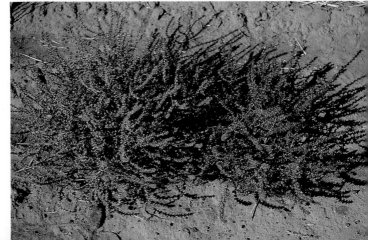

GRASS FAMILY Gramineae

The grasses constitute the single most important group of plants in the sagebrush steppe. They are indispensable as the major food source for nearly all herbivorous inhabitants, including cattle. As dominant representatives of steppe communities grasses have a major influence on the structure of those communities. They are instrumental in preventing or inhibiting soil erosion and participate in the stabilization of dunes. They provide shelter for various small animals and serve a number of lesser roles. Like all large families, however, the *Gramineae* is not without its villains. Some of the most successful weeds are grasses. Many species produce "seeds" that become lodged in the mouths of grazing animals. Some introduced species are very aggressive and thrive in the steppe at the expense of native grasses and other plants. Finally, all grasses are "villains" in that they are wind pollinated and produce large masses of air-borne pollen over long periods of time. The respondents are, of course, the thousands of hay fever victims.

Strategies of adaptation exploited by grasses are both numerous and effective. The evolution of elaborate anatomical and structural characteristics has enabled grasses to absorb and conserve water efficiently. In addition, most species can tolerate extensive dehydration without permanent tissue damage. Finally, many species are short-lived annuals that complete their life cycle (from seed to seed) during moist periods, thus escaping drought. Unquestionably, no similarly large group of plants is as well adapted to the semiarid conditions of the steppe as the grasses.

Grasses have also evolved an efficient system of wind pollination. The sepals and petals, which can only interfere with the transfer of pollen by wind, have been lost. At the time of pollen release, the stamens elongate until they extend well beyond confining bracts, thus enabling the pollen to freely disperse in the wind. At the same time, the sticky, pollen-receptive, feathery stigmas become completely exposed and "comb" the air for pollen grains.

In spite of extensive and obvious differences among most species, grasses generally tend to look alike, making some basis for the statement, "if you've seen one grass you've seen them all" or "a grass is a grass is a grass...." The leaves are primarily basal and tufted, and are long, narrow, and parallel-veined. The round and jointed stems arise from extensively branched root systems or from creeping underground stems called rhizomes. The flowers consist only of stamens and/or pistils and are associated with various chaff-like bracts that often have hair-like or bristle-like appendages (awns). The flower(s) and associated bracts collectively form a spikelet, which may be borne directly on the stem, as with wheat, or on flexuous branches, as with oats. The fruit is, of course, a grain. Any comprehensive treatment of steppe vegetation would necessarily include discussion of numerous species of grasses. However, only a few of the most important representatives are considered here.

Bluebunch wheatgrass
Agropyron spicatum

Blue grama *Bouteloua*

Steppe bluegrass *Poa secunda*

Bluebunch wheatgrass (*Agropyron spicatum*) is one of the most important forage grasses of the steppe. This rather tall (up to three feet) bunch grass produces numerous slender stems, each with a narrow terminal spike. It grows as a common and often conspicuous dominant in the more moist regions, particularly in areas of deep soil accumulation. Most of the wheatgrass (bunch grass) prairies are now under cultivation.

Steppe bluegrass (*Poa secunda*) is one of several poorly distinguished bluegrasses. It forms small clumps with narrow, short leaves and slender stems with many small spikelets on short upright branches. Steppe bluegrass inhabits thinner, drier soils than bluebunch wheatgrass, often growing on lithosols.

Idaho fescue (*Festuca idahoensis*) resembles steppe bluegrass but is taller and forms larger clumps with numerous round, bluish leaves. It has bristle-like awns in the spikelets, and grows in deeper, more moist soils, often in association with ponderosa pine.

Cheat grass (*Bromus tectorum*) is an introduced annual that has become distributed throughout the steppe. It competes successfully with native species, especially in overgrazed or otherwise disturbed areas. Cheat grass produces characteristic large, nodding spikelets with long, firm, bristle-like awns.

Indian rice grass (*Oryzopsis hymenoides*) is an attractive bunch grass with a diffusely branched, feathery crown. It is very important in the stabilization of dunes. Another grass that favors sandy soil is **needle grass** (*Stipa comata*), which has very long, twisted, needle-like awns.

Giant wild rye (*Elymus cinereus*) is a very coarse and tall (up to six feet) grass that grows in large bunches, usually in relatively moist, slightly alkaline flats. This grass has dense spikes that resemble wheat. In salt flats, it is replaced by the low, **creeping salt grass** (*Distichlis stricta*).

In Colorado and the eastern extreme of the sagebrush zone, the **blue grama** (*Bouteloua*) and **buffalo** (*Buchloe*) grasses become the most important range grasses. These two species do not form clumps as bunch grasses do, but spread by runners or rhizomes. They are sod-formers. The spikelets on both of these attractive grasses are concentrated on one side of the spike.

A frequent associate of the blue grama in the shortgrass prairie is **prairie junegrass** (*Koeleria cristata*) which produces short, rather dense inflorescences. The spikelets have either short awns or no awns.

Idaho fescue   *Festuca idahoensis*   **Prairie junegrass   *Koeleria cristata***

Cheat grass   *Bromus tectorum*
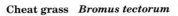

IRIS FAMILY

Iridaceae

Flowers of the iris family follow the floral "formula" of parts occuring in sets of three: three sepals, three petals, three stamens and three styles. The sepals and petals are usually similar in size, shape and color. The iris family differs from the lily family by having three rather than six stamens and an inferior rather than superior ovary.

Wild iris, flag

Iris missouriensis

The wild iris is a strikingly beautiful plant that forms small but dense populations that spread by rootstalks (rhizomes). As the populations increase in diameter, the central, older individuals often die, leaving an outer ring of plants. The stems are one to two feet tall within several grass-like leaves of approximately equal height. The showy flowers have three drooping blue sepals, two to three inches long, usually with purplish lines; three erect, somewhat smaller petals; and three blue style branches that are flattened and petal-like. The fruit is a large capsule.

Wild iris grows throughout the steppeland in meadows or low areas that are wet or moist in the spring but may dry out later in the year. Sometimes when other food sources are unavailable, cattle feed on the leaves and stems of wild iris, only to be afflicted with a "belly-ache." The rootstalks, especially, contain a toxic material, irisin, which can be lethal if eaten. Plains Indians reportedly used this toxin in a mixture of bile as an arrowhead poison.

Iris is the Greek word for rainbow. Presumably this genus was given the name because of its showy flowers of a variety of bright colors. In *Iris missouriensis* the flower color varies from a very pale blue to dark blue or bluish-purple.

Grass widow

Sisyrinchium species

Three species of grass widow (or blue-eyed grass) have limited distribution in the sagebrush steppe. All require similar habitat-moist spring conditions in the high plains or open forests-and all combinations apparently hybridize when their ranges overlap.

Grass widows flower early in the spring, then become "hidden" because of their grass-like appearance among the steppe vegetation. The flowers are borne singly or in small clusters on the flattened stems, at the base of one or more sheathing leaves. The flower parts come in threes: three sepals, three petals, three stamens, and three compartments in the ovary.

The most widespread and variable of the grass widows is *Sisyrinchium angustifolium*, which formerly has been divided into a number of species. It has comparatively small, blue flowers and appears sporadically in suitable habitats throughout the steppeland and adjacent ponderosa pine forests and piñon-juniper woodlands. The most attractive species is *S. douglasii*, a grass widow with relatively large, purple flowers. This plant grows in Washington, Oregon, and California. The third species, *S. inflatum*, is a similar but smaller-flowered plant that extends from the Cascade and Sierra Ranges to eastern Idaho and northern Utah.

Wild iris   *Iris missouriensis*

Grass widow   *Sisyrinchium*

Grass widow   *Sisyrinchium*

LILY FAMILY　　　　　Liliaceae

Most species of this family combine characteristics that easily identify them as "lilies." Sepals and petals are usually similar in shape, size, and color and appear in sets of three. The plants have six stamens and a superior ovary with three stigmas and three internal compartments. Most plants produce bulbs and long, grass-like leaves. The lily family provides some of the most beautiful wildflowers of the sagebrush steppe. Some are occasionally collected because of their edibility, some are deadly poisonous.

Mariposa or sego lily　　　*Calochortus* species

As the Greek derivation of the generic name indicates (*Kalo* means beautiful, *chorta* means grass), the species of Calochortus are unusually attractive. Their characteristic three broad, lavender to white petals usually bear a patch of hair-like filaments on the inner surface near the base and an associated purple band or splotch. Below the hairy band lies a conspicuous green or yellow gland, sunken into the base of the petal. The stems, un-branched below the flower stalks, arise from round starchy bulbs to bear a few to several rather thick but grass-like leaves. The flowers are typical of lilies with three sepals, three petals and six stamens. They are atypical in that the petals are larger, more ornate, and more brightly colored than the sepals. Unfortunately, the beauty of the flowers has led to over-collection and commercial exploitation of some species to the extent that they are now endangered.

The showiest species, at least in terms of size, is **mariposa lily** (***Calochortus macrocarpus***), a tall plant with one to three large, pale to dark lavender flowers. The narrow sepals, approximately two inches long, are somewhat longer than the broad, greenish-striped petals. Mariposa lily grows in dry sandy soil often in major river drainages where it suffers from grazing pressure as well as from collection. It is irregularly distributed over the western "half" of the sagebrush steppe.

A very common species in the eastern "half" of the steppeland is **sego lily** (***Calochortus nuttallii***), the state flower of Utah. It displays a conspicuous red to purple band over a bright yellow "eyebrow" complete with long hairs. The eyebrow is appropriately positioned above the eye-like yellow gland. The white petals, about an inch long and wide, are fan-shaped with an abrupt point in the center.

Cats-ear (*Calochortus lyallii*) is a smaller but equally attractive lily, widely distributed in high sagebrush prairies and lower forests of eastern Washington and adjacent British Columbia. Its ear-shaped petals bordered by long hairs distinguish cats-ear. It has a purple, hairy "eyebrow" above the conspicuous sunken, green gland.

Mariposa lily   *Calochortus macrocarpus*

Sego lily   *Calochortus nuttallii*

Cats-ear   *Calochortus lyallii*

Wild onion

Allium species

Wild onions are both numerous and generally difficult to distinguish. All are herbaceous plants with basal, grass-like leaves and round or elongate bulbs. The flowers form an attractive umbrella-like or head-like cluster at the tip of the stem. Each flower produces a combination of three petals and three sepals more or less similar in shape (elliptical and sharp-tipped), size (up to 1/2 inch long), and color (white to shades of red and purple). Occasionally, small bulbs replace the flowers.

The various wild onions are widespread and frequently form dense populations that provide a very showy and colorful display of pink to purple or white blooms during the flowering season. Like cultivated onions, the wild forms easily stand out with their onion- or garlic-like odor and taste. The genus gets its name from the Latin word *allium*, which means garlic. All species are edible and make excellent garlic butter or add flavor to stews.

The most common and widespread of the wild onions is ***Allium acuminatum***, which grows more or less throughout the sagebrush steppe. The flower color varies somewhat but is most frequently rose-purple. The two to three grooved leaves usually wither away by the time the flowers appear.

One of the most attractive of the wild onions is ***Allium douglasii*** with pink, star-shaped flowers. Frequently it forms dense populations, odorous but spectacular. This highly variable species commonly inhabits the steppes of Washington, Oregon and Idaho. It produces two grooved leaves that persist through the flowering period.

One of the rarest of the wild onions is ***Allium robinsonii***, restricted to basaltic outcrops along the Columbia River in central Washington and adjacent Oregon. This unusual, weak-stemmed plant lies flat across its rocky substrate. The flowers are white to very pale lilac. The succulent, flattened leaves persist through the flowering period.

Wild onion *Allium acuminatum*

Wild onion *Allium douglasii*
Wild onion *Allium robinsonii*

Brodiaea

Brodiaea douglasii

With the exception of some of the wild onions, this species is the most widespread and populous lily of the sagebrush steppe. It also commonly grows in piñon-juniper woodlands, in open ponderosa pine forests, and along rocky, montane ridges. Although the flowers of brodiaea (also called wild hyacinth) are showy, the plants themselves are unattractive. Each has a deeply buried, flattish, fibrous-coated bulb; a tall (up to three feet), thin, flexuous stem with an umbrella-like cluster of several flowers; and one or two grass-like leaves nearly as long as the stem, borne from the bulb below ground level. The flowers vary in color from pale to dark blue and fuse at the base to form a broad tube with six lobes (three petals and three sepals), each with wavy margins.

Two additional species of Brodiaea inhabit the steppeland: *Brodiaea howellii*, a common plant along the western "edge" of the steppe, and *Brodiaea hyacinthina*, an occasional plant in the western "half" of the steppe. Both have whitish, or pale blue flowers, and in the latter species the floral tube is much shorter than the lobes. All three brodiaeas prefer relatively deep, sandy soils in moderately dry sites. Like those of onions, brodiaea bulbs are edible and have a nut-like flavor when cooked. They were eaten extensively by Indians and early settlers.

Yellow bell

Fritillaria pudica

One of the most unforgettable characters of sagebrush country is the beautiful yellow bell. Undoubtedly, its popularity relates in part to the fact that it flowers in very early spring when the desolate recesses of winter linger over the drab countryside. Frequent and colorful spring flowering associates of yellow bell are spring beauty (*Claytonia lanceolata*), salt and pepper (*Lomatium gormanii*), and sagebrush buttercup (*Ranunculus glaberrimus*).

Like other lilies, yellow bell bears floral parts in multiples of three, and the sepals and petals are similar in color and form. The individual plants arise from a bulb with numerous smaller rice-like bulblets (accordingly, the genus is often called riceroot). The leaves, elongate and fleshy, grow in pairs or in whorls of three or more near mid-height on the stem. The bright yellow, nodding, bell-shaped flowers are borne singly or in pairs at the stem tip and become orangish with age. The capsule resembles a dice box, and this likeness is responsible for the generic name (in Latin, *fritill* means dice box). *Pudica* is Latin for ashamed or bashful and relates to the flower's nodding habit.

The yellow bell is common in the high plains and open forests of western North America, in areas with sufficient spring moisture. It also commonly grows along rocky ridges in the mountains. Here, too, it is usually associated with sagebrush.

Brodiaea   *Brodiaea douglasii*

Brodiaea   *Brodiaea howellii*
Yellow bell   *Fritillaria pudica*

Leopard lily   *Fritillaria atropurpurea*

This unusual lily tends to be overlooked because of its well-camouflaged, nodding flowers. The sepals and petals are greenish-yellow with purple spots or splotches. The leafy stems stand up to one and a half feet tall. Leopard lily grows throughout the Rocky Mountain area of the sagebrush steppe, extending well up into the mountains.

Camas   *Camassia quamash*

Camas is a beautiful plant with large and congested, pale blue to dark purplish-blue flowers. As is true of most lilies, the sepals and petals are of similar color and size (about one inch long), and the flower parts come in multiples of three: three sepals, three petals, six stamens, and three compartments in the ovary. Stems usually reach one to two feet tall, have a few fleshy, grass-like leaves with parallel veins, and are derived from starchy bulbs.

The names "camas" and "quamash" were given to this plant by Indians who relied upon the bulbs as a source of food. Early settlers also used the bulbs as a food supplement, and even today Indians, especially Nez Perce, and other people regularly collect and eat camas bulbs. Camas grows in meadows or low, non-salty areas that are wet in the spring. Often it forms vast populations, such as in the Camas Prairie near Lewiston, Idaho, that appear from the hills above as seas of blue during the spring flowering period. Camas is extremely variable and occupies a wide range of suitable habitats throughout western North America.

Death camas   *Zygadenus venenosus*

Death camas is a common associate of sagebrush over much of the steppeland. This typical liliaceous plant produces long, rather thick, parallel-veined leaves from a slightly elongate bulb that buries itself progressively deeper as the plant ages. The flowers form a rather dense pyramidal cluster that becomes more elongate, and the individual flowers more widely spaced, as flowering progresses. The three sepals and three petals are white or more commonly cream-colored to pale yellow. The fruit develops into a three lobed capsule.

Death camas contains an alkaloid poisonous to livestock, particularly sheep. Also, people who have eaten the bulbs as a result of mistaken identity have suffered accordingly. An interesting aspect of the poisonous nature of death camas relates to its nectar. Experiments have demonstrated that honeybees can be fatally poisoned from feeding on the nectar. It seems, therefore, that the poisonous property has created a conflict of interest for death camas, it protects against herbivores but restricts pollinators.

Leopard lily *Fritillaria atropurpurea*

Camas *Camassia quamash*

Camas *Camassia quamash*

Death camas *Zygadenus venenosus*

LOASA FAMILY
Loasaceae

This is a small family with a single genus (*Mentzelia*) but a great deal of variation among the species, from small inconspicuous annuals to showy perennials. The most outstanding characteristic of the family is the numerous stamens in combination with an inferior ovary.

Blazing star
Mentzelia laeviculmis

Blazing star injects great beauty into the usually drab setting of the mid- or late summer steppeland. Its brilliant, lemon-yellow flowers are large and showy with five or more widely spreading, sharply pointed petals that collectively form a nearly perfect star. The many stamens, also yellow, project forward from the center of the "star," giving it a blazing appearance. The sepals are very narrow, somewhat shorter than and alternate with the two-inch petals. With age the sepals become twisted and leathery, remaining as appendages on the mature, somewhat woody, capsular fruit. The whitish stems are branched with alternate, deeply lobed leaves. Very harsh, barbed, sandpaper-like hair covers both the stems and leaves.

Blazing star is a short-lived, occasional plant on fine talus slopes and gravelly sagebrush plains. It is particularly conspicuous because of its attractiveness and its distribution along cut-banks and gravel shoulders of highways.

Blazing star *Mentzelia laeviculmis*

Blazing star *Mentzelia laeviculmis*

MALLOW FAMILY   Malvaceae

World-wide, the mallow family is very large and diverse, including such well-known plants as cotton, hibiscus, and hollyhock. The two most useful identifying characteristics of the family are the numerous stamens fused at the base to form a tube around the style, and the fruit that separates into single-seeded, pie-shaped segments at maturity.

Orange globe mallow   *Sphaeralcea munroana*

The unusual orange coloration of its flowers make orange globe mallow a conspicuous and easily recognized species. The five colorful petals, approximately 1/2 inch long, overlap somewhat to collectively form an attractive "bowl" containing the numerous stamens. The leaves are dark green to somewhat grayish, due to a dense covering of minute, star-shaped hairs, and palmately-lobed like those of geraniums. The widely branched plants arise from a very deep and strong woody root system.

The orange globe mallow is an extremely adaptable and widely distributed species. It grows in many different soil types but prefers moderately sandy or rocky sites. It lives throughout the ecological extreme of the sagebrush steppe and extends southward into the drier Sonoran and Mojave Deserts. In the Great Basin, this species is largely replaced by the similar **scarlet globe mallow (*Sphaeralcea coccinea*)**, which has somewhat redder (to scarlet) flowers and more deeply divided leaves.

The generic name comes from Greek: *sphaera* means globe-like and refers to the round fruit with pie-shaped segments; *alcea* means mallow.

Orange globe mallow   *Sphaeralcea munroana*

Scarlet globe mallow   *Sphaeralcea coccinea*

MINT FAMILY

Labiatae

The mint family includes a number of shrubs, some spiny, and several species of perennial herbs. The most important family characteristics are square stems with opposite leaves; highly ornate, bilaterally symmetrical flowers; and a four-lobed ovary that matures into four one-seeded nutlets. Most species emit a very strong minty or sage odor.

Purple sage

Salvia dorrii

Purple sage is a conspicuous low to medium-sized shrub easily recognized by its very strong minty-sage odor and elegant, fragrant, blue-violet flowers. It is symmetrical and extensively branched, with numerous narrow, thickened, opposite leaves. Flowers are borne in whorls at the ends of upright branches and are associated with thickened purplish bracts. The petals' elaborate design allows for bee pollination with a basal, nectar-containing tube, a broad, lobed lower lip or landing platform, two lateral lobes and two upright lobes. The two stamens and style brush the bee's back when she enters the flower.

Purple sage most frequently inhabits partially stabilized talus slopes, rock outcrops, or rocky plains, and often is a dominant member of its community. It is irregularly distributed from eastern Washington and Oregon south and east through southern Idaho and Nevada to Utah.

Skullcap

Scutellaria species

The most distinctive characteristic of this genus is an erect appendage on the back of the tubular (fused) sepals. The Latin name, *scutella*, means tray and refers to this appendage. The appendage forms a fanciful skull cap.

Most skullcaps grow in moist areas, especially along the banks of streams. However the **snapdragon skullcap (*Scutellaria antirrhinoides*)** frequently occupies dry, often rocky habitats, from the prairies well up into the mountains. It bears blue-purple, snapdragon-like flowers with the entrance to the floral tube closed. Only a clever bee can access the floral rewards. This skullcap is primarily a Great Basin species, distributed from northern California to Utah. It flowers in late spring.

Purple sage   *Salvia dorrii*

Purple sage
Salvia dorrii

Snapdragon skullcap
Scutellaria antirrhinoides

87

MUSTARD FAMILY Cruciferae

The Cruciferae is a large and variable family, but the numerous species share several "mustard" characteristics. Most important among these is the floral "formula": four sepals, four petals, and six stamens. The fruit typically is a two-compartmented pod, the compartments separated by a papery partition that remains on the flower stalk after the seeds disperse. The species vary from minute annuals to medium-sized shrubs. Leaves are alternate and often pinnately compound.

Prince's plume *Stanleya pinnata*

Prince's plume is a rather striking inhabitant of the southern and drier areas of the sagebrush steppe. This tall plant, often exceeding three feet, produces several unbranched stems, each with a terminal, plume-like cluster of small, bright-yellow flowers. The basal leaves are pinnately divided or compound and soon dry out and fall off. The smaller, undivided, upper leaves persist longer. Like other flowers of the mustard family, each bloom has four sepals and four petals. The fruit is long and narrow.

Prince's plume accumulates selenium from the soil and substitutes it for sulfur in some of its amino acids. The plant tolerates or even benefits by this substitution but animals do not. The chemically and functionally altered amino acids and proteins are highly toxic to livestock and wildlife. Fortunately, the plants are seldom eaten.

Prince's plume is widely distributed in the dry, sandy sagebrush plains and talus slopes of northern Nevada and Utah, southern Idaho and Wyoming, and northeastern Oregon. Its broad ecological range extends from the dry, sandy soils of the Mojave Desert to the high, juniper-covered ridges of Colorado.

Thelypodium *Thelypodium laciniatum*

Thelypodium is a rather tall and thick-stemmed, biennial herb with a radish-like taproot. The stems usually have several, strictly erect branches, terminating in a dense, spire-like cluster, or raceme, of flowers and/or fruits. The flowers bear four greenish-white or occasionally purplish sepals and four narrow, white, half-inch petals. The long and narrow fruits develop from the bottom of the raceme upward. The fleshy leaves are variously toothed and divided and concentrate near the base of the stems.

Thelypodium is widespread in the deserts and steppes of western North America. It most frequently inhabits sandy sagebrush plains and talus slopes. It flowers in early summer.

Prince's plume, community scene
(Stanleya pinnata)

Thelypodium
Thelypodium laciniatum

Prince's plume   *Stanleya pinnata*

Tumble mustard
Sisymbrium altissimum

The unattractive tumble mustard, whose scientific name means "very tall and sweet-smelling," is a widespread weed of European origin. It grows chiefly in disturbed areas, particularly those with loose, sandy soil. This rather tall (up to three feet), much-branched annual produces pinnately compound or divided lower leaves and reduced upper ones. The small, pale yellow flowers give rise to long, linear, pod-like fruits. The entire plant presents a somewhat circular profile; after death it uproots and rolls in the wind, spreading its seeds as it tumbles.

This plant should not be confused with Russian thistle, also a tumbleweed. Tumble mustard is more sparsely branched, has a light straw color, and lacks the spininess of the widespread Russian thistle.

Dagger-pod
Phoenicaulis cheiranthoides

Dagger-pod is a distinctive plant with a thick, woody rootcrown bearing many narrowly elliptical leaves and several leafless stems. The stems are sometimes erect but more often spread out to form a broad ring around the central leaves. The pink to reddish flowers are borne in a congested raceme along the upper or outer half of the stem. The fruits mature into dagger-like pods that project outward at right angles from the stem on short stalks, called pedicels. The stem is often reddish-colored and presumably the generic name relates to this trait: in Greek *phoeni* means reddish-purple and *caulis* means stems. *Cheiranthoides* translates as a hand of flowers.

Dagger-pod inhabits the high plains and open forests of eastern Washington and Oregon and adjacent Nevada and Idaho. It grows in rocky, thin soils (lithosols), flowering in early spring.

Prairie rocket
Erysimum asperum

Wallflower, the common name for the genus *Erysimum*, also is frequently applied to this species. By any name, this is one of the most attractive members of the large mustard family. The numerous showy flowers have four sepals, four bright yellow petals, and six stamens. Each petal, about one inch long, has a broad, flat blade and a very narrow base, or claw. The plants usually produce several stems, which vary in height from six to 36 inches. The many narrow, often toothed leaves concentrate mainly at the base of the stem. The flowers form a terminal, rather dense cluster, or raceme, and the fruits are long and very narrow.

Prairie rocket grows throughout the sagebrush steppe, from southern British Columbia south into California and east to the prairies of Wyoming and Colorado. It prefers sandy plains but extends upward into the fine gravelly slopes of the alpine.

A similar species with a more restricted distribution is western wallflower (*Erysimum occidentale*), which grows in the steppes of Washington, Oregon, Idaho and Nevada.

Tumble mustard
Sisymbrium altissimum

Prairie rocket
Erysimum asperum

Dagger-pod   *Phoenicaulis cheiranthoides*

Bladder-pods   *Physaria* and *Lesquerella* species

The bladder-pods are low mustards with bright yellow flowers. The fruit matures into a round or two-lobed pod, which in many species inflates bladder-like. Each pod has a single, narrow style.

Both *Lesquerella* and *Physaria* produce several weak, spreading stems and numerous leaves, most derived from the woody rootcrown. Typical for mustards, each flower has four sepals, four petals, and six stamens. The very dense, star-shaped hairs that cover the stems, leaves, pods, and sepals of these two genera give the plants a grayish cast. The subtleties of these hairs cannot be appreciated without a microscope.

Species of *Lesquerella* and *Physaria* appear to intergrade and apparently hybridize when their ranges overlap. Both genera are widely represented in the sagebrush steppe and favor gravelly slopes and plains.

Rock cress   *Arabis* species

Several species of rock cress inhabit the sagebrush steppe, some very common and widespread. Most species have white or pale lavender flowers. The four sepals and four petals tightly enclose the ovary and stamens, giving the flower a tubular appearance. Stems usually grow upright and unbranched with a whorl of basal leaves and a few to several "clasping" stem leaves with basal ear-like lobes that project from the sides of the stem. The individual flowers have short stalks, or pedicels, creating narrow and elongate flower clusters called racemes. The narrow (linear) fruits split open at maturity. Typically, the stems and leaves are covered with branched or star-shaped hairs that can only be observed with a microscope.

Probably the most widespread and variable species of rock cress is *Arabis holboellii* with white or pink flowers and drooping fruits. One of the most attractive species is **Arabis divaricarpa** with reddish-purple flowers. It grows in the high plains and mountains of the western "half" of the sagebrush steppe.

Bladder-pod *Lesquerella douglasii*

Rock cress *Arabis divaricarpa*

Bladder-pod *Physaria vitulifera*

PARSLEY FAMILY Umbelliferae

The most outstanding characteristic of the Umbelliferae is the inflorescence consisting of one to, more frequently, several umbrella-like flower clusters called umbels. The individual flowers are small, with five petals, five stamens, and no sepals. The inferior ovary matures into a dry, two-seeded fruit. The leaves are compound and often fern-like. Although the family is large, most species grow only in moist or wet habitats.

Desert parsley *Lomatium* species

Several species of Lomatium, many of which are extremely common, inhabit the sagebrush steppe. All have divided, fern-like or carrot-like leaves (although in some species the leaf segments are rather large), and all produce very small flowers crowded into several umbrella-like clusters. In most species the flowers are yellow. The often-flat fruits have thin "winged" edges responsible for the generic name (*loma* means wing or border in Greek).

Although certainly not one of the more conspicuous species, **salt & pepper** (***Lomatium gormanii***) offers its own special kind of beauty. This is largely because it is one of the first plants to flower in the spring when the steppe is still "dressed in its drab winter uniform." It has dark purple anthers (pepper) sprinkled over the white petals (salt). The leaves divide into several long, narrow segments. Salt & pepper inhabits the steppes and montane ridges west of the Continental Divide.

The most robust of all the desert parsleys is **fern-leaf desert parsley** (***Lomatium dissectum***), a highly variable species with a broad range. This desert parsley grows as much as four feet tall. The leaves, mostly basal, are large and fern-like, that is, divided into many small segments. The multiple umbels develop on a long, leafless stalk, with flowers that vary in color from deep purple, nearly black, to pale yellow. The white anthers contrast sharply with the petals in the purple-flowered form. Considering all the varieties, fern-leaf desert parsley is distributed throughout the sagebrush steppe. It most frequently grows in rocky habitats, particularly on talus slopes.

Perhaps the most common, strictly yellow-flowered species is **nine-leaved desert parsley (*Lomatium triternatum*)**. Leaves with three sets of three long, narrow segments (triternate) mark this species. The mostly leafless stems stand up to two feet tall. The compact umbels cluster to form a larger, flat-topped umbel. This species, in its many varietal forms, grows throughout the sagebrush steppe, usually in habitats that are particularly moist in the spring but that dry by early summer.

Salt & pepper *Lomatium gormanii*

Fern-leaf desert parsley
Lomatium dissectum

Nine-leaved desert parsley
Lomatium triternatum

95

Many species of Lomatium have fleshy tuberous or bulb-like roots that can be beaten or ground into "flour" for making bread-type foods. From this use, certain species within this genus have come to be known as "biscuitroot." These plants provided an important food source for Plains Indians, and many people continue to collect and eat the plants today. The leaves have a parsley-like flavor, though often very strong. This flavor, together with the divided leaves and desert distribution, give the genus its common name.

One of the species that most deserves the common name of parsley is **Gray's desert parsley (*Lomatium grayi*)**. The leaves of this plant divide into numerous small segments and the plants give off a very strong, rather unpleasant, parsley-like odor. However, the plants produce very attractive dark green, divided leaves and bright yellow flowers borne in tight umbels on leafless stems. This species grows more or less throughout the sagebrush steppe, usually preferring coarse, rocky habitats, such as talus slopes or dry, rocky ravines.

One of the least attractive of the Lomatium species is **large-fruited biscuitroot (*Lomatium macrocarpum*)**. Its very dense, ball-like umbels contain greenish-white (or occasionally purplish-white) flowers. The short flowering stems spread laterally rather than stand erect. The leaves, clumped at the base and center of the plant, are a grayish color due to short dense pubescence. The fruits are relatively large, dime-size, and flattened. This species has thick, tuberous roots that have historically been used as a flour substitute, thus the common name of biscuitroot. Frustratingly, the plants usually grow in very rocky habitats, such as lithosols, making it very difficult to harvest the roots. Distribution includes most of the sagebrush steppe.

The most distinctive of the *Lomatium* species is **bare-stem desert parsley (*Lomatium nudicaule*)**. The leaves—its distinctive trait—are pinnately compound with toothed, oval leaf segments usually more than an inch long and nearly as wide. As the common and specific epithet suggest, the flowering stems lack leaves (*nudi* means naked, *caule* means stem). This desert parsley grows throughout the sagebrush steppe except in the eastern extremes.

Gray's desert parsley   *Lomatium grayi*

Large-fruited biscuitroot   *Lomatium macrocarpum*
Bare-stem desert parsley   *Lomatium nudicaule*

Yampah   *Perideridia* species

Yampah is a delicate and attractive plant. Its leaves are divided into long and very narrow segments. Its minute, white flowers occur in dense, round-topped clusters formed by several small umbels. The entire plant presents a somewhat lacy appearance.

Yampah was named by Plains Indians who collected the plant's elongate, starchy bulbs, usually two per plant. The bulbs were, and still are, eaten fresh, cooked, dried, or ground into flour and used for baking. With a definite carrot flavor, yampah is one of the most nourishing and savory wild plants. The generic name comes from the Greek *perideri*, which means necklace. How the name relates to this plant is not clear.

Yampah often forms extensive populations in high moist plains and sagebrush slopes in the mountains. Frequently it grows in open conifer or aspen forests, ranging upward to subalpine meadows. It flowers throughout the summer months, the leaves drying up and falling off late in the season.

Yampah *Perideridia gairdneri*

Yampah *Perideridia gairdneri*

PEA FAMILY
Leguminosae

Very well represented in the sagebrush steppe, the pea family is both large and ecologically important. Frequently, members of the legume family become dominants in their respective communities. They provide a source of protein-rich foliage and seeds for many animals, and legumes enrich the soil by fixing nitrogen. However, many legumes are at least mildly poisonous, some deadly.

The family is highly variable, including everything from small annuals to large trees. However, characteristics of the flowers and fruit create a unifying theme. The fruit forms a pod, usually with a single compartment and several seeds, like a pea pod. The bilaterally symmetrical flowers consist of an upper petal (the banner), two lateral petals (the wings), and two lower petals which are usually at least partially fused (the keel). The ten stamens and the style are "spring loaded" inside the keel and release forcefully when an insect, usually a bee, depresses the keel. In this way pollen is both deposited on the insect and picked up instantaneously. Another identifying family characteristic is the leaf type; with few exceptions, legumes have compound leaves.

Locoweed
Astragalus species

Within the sagebrush steppe, no other genus contains as many species as *Astragalus*, many very similar and difficult to distinguish. Still, within the genus as a whole there is considerable variation. Most species grow as low, spreading plants, but some may be more than two feet tall. The flowers, although all generally pea-like, vary considerably in size and color. As is true of all legumes, the fruit is a pod, but there is little uniformity in its nature and size. Most plants have pinnately compound leaves, but the size and shape of the leaflets varies between species. Finally, the numerous species show a wide range of ecological adaptations. However, most grow in rather dry, open areas, and the steppeland appears to provide ideal habitats. This is especially true in and around Wyoming where locoweeds are most prevalent.

Three of the many important species of *Astragalus* are *A. bisulcatus*, **Woolly-pod locoweed (*A. purshii*)**, and *A. miser*. *A. bisulcatus* is a tall, many-stemmed plant with elongate clusters of white or violet flowers. It is very common and conspicuous in the sagebrush plains of the Rocky Mountain region. Woolly-pod locoweed is a low and dense cushion plant with colorful, usually reddish purple, flowers and white-woolly pods. It grows throughout the sagebrush steppe in rocky, thin soils (lithosols). *A. miser* is a highly variable, low plant with short clusters of white and purplish flowers and narrow, straight pods. It grows more or less throughout the steppe. A common sand-loving species in Washington and Oregon is **crouching locoweed (*A. succumbens*)**. It produces head-like racemes of large lavender-purple flowers and narrow, straight pods. Crouching locoweed prefers sandy areas of eastern Washington and Oregon. A widespread, erect species with narrow leaflets and white to cream-colored flowers is **hanging-pod locoweed (*Astragalus arrectus*)**. This plant ranges from eastern Washington through the steppes of Idaho and Montana, especially on hillsides along the major rivers.

Woolly-pod locoweed *Astragalus purshii*

Crouching locoweed *Astragalus succumbens*

Hanging-pod locoweed *Astragalus arrectus*

Although the flowers of locoweeds vary in size, shape, and color (from white to shades of red and purple), the pods prove most useful in distinguishing species. Some pods stand erect, others hang down. Some are very narrow and elongate, others resemble grapes more than pods. Some are densely woolly or otherwise hairy, others are hairless. Some pods are straight, others hooked or coiled. Two species that exemplify the extremes in pod shape are **buffalo plum locoweed (*Astragalus crassicarpus*)**, with nearly round, grape-like pods, and **thread-stalk locoweed (*Astragalus filipes*)**, with long, flattened pods. The former is common in the eastern "half" of the steppe, the latter in the western "half."

Locoweeds represent a dual threat in terms of livestock poisoning. Several species have the ability to accumulate large amounts of selenium, which upsets the protein metabolism of animals that eat the plants. This causes acute poisoning and often death. In addition, many or most species contain an alkaloid-like substance, "locine." The effects of locine are cumulative and large amounts of the plants must be eaten, often over a period of several days, before the symptoms begin to show. Normally animals avoid locoweed unless food is scarce, but many get "hooked" or develop the "loco habit." The disease gets its name from the associated symptoms of lack of coordination and muscular control, coupled, with violent and unpredictable behavior when aroused. Animals rarely recover completely after having suffered from loco poisoning.

A closely related genus of similar distribution, *Oxytropis*, can usually be distinguished by its lack of stem leaves; the leaves all rise directly from the rootcrown. Species of this genus posess poisonous properties similar to *Astragalus* and are called crazyweed (or locoweed also). The two most widespread species are **silver crazyweed (*Oxytropis sericeus*)** and **rabbit-foot crazyweed (*Oxytropis lagopus*)** both common in the high plains of the eastern steppe, extending westward into Idaho and Nevada. Fine hairs cover silver crazyweed, giving it a silvery hue. It has white to pale yellow flowers occasionally tinted with lavender. Fuzzy sepals that fancifully resemble a rabbit's foot give *O. lagopus* its common name. It has bright lavender-purple flowers.

Buffalo plum locoweed
Astragalus crassicarpus

Thread-stalk locoweed
Astragalus filipes

Silver crazyweed   *Oxytropis sericeus*

Rabbit-foot crazyweed   *Oxytropis lagopus*

103

Lupine   *Lupinus* species

Some of the most frequent associates of sagebrush are the various species of lupine, often difficult to distinguish from each other but clearly distinct from other genera. The most outstanding characteristic of lupines is the palmately-compound leaves with four to eight elongate leaflets all derived from the same point on the leaf stalk. The pea-like lupine flowers are usually blue and white or occasionally yellowish in rather dense, head-like or, more frequently, elongate clusters, called racemes, at the tip of hollow stems or branches. Dense hair covers most plants, a water-retaining adaptation.

Like other legumes, lupines fix nitrogen, thus making a significant ecological contribution to the steppe, particularly to nitrogen-deficient sandy soils. They are also important in a negative way because they contain poisonous alkaloids. Livestock poisoning frequently occurs when hungry animals, particularly sheep, are trailed through lupine populations where they feed on the toxic seeds and pod-like fruits.

Many species of lupine grow scattered over the sagebrush steppe, some sporadic in occurrence, some widespread and frequently dominant members of their steppe community. Probably the most common and widespread species is **prairie lupine** (*Lupinus wyethii*) pictured on page viii and 109. Lupines usually inhabit the high plains and mountains, but some species are sufficiently drought tolerant to live in the desert. Most species prefer deep, sandy soils; a few grow only on lithosols.

Of the many species, only a few can be discussed here. They have been selected as geographical representatives of the genus as well as examples of color variation.

Dry-ground lupine (*Lupinus aridus*) is a distinctive, compact, cushion plant of dry, rocky, thin soils (lithosols). The flowers, blue (or violet) and white (rarely totally white), form dense elliptical clusters partially hidden by the leaves. This is an early flowering lupine of Washington, Oregon and Idaho, ranging south into Nevada and California.

Sulphur lupine (*Lupinus sulphureus*) is one of a few lupines with white (cream-colored) or pale yellow flowers. This medium-sized, branched plant lives in the gravelly soils of the high plains of Washington, Oregon, and California.

Foothills lupine (*Lupinus ammophilus*) is one of the most attractive lupines of the steppe, with its showy racemes of blue-violet and white flowers. It grows in the high plains of Utah and Colorado, extending eastward into the shortgrass prairie.

104

Dry-ground lupine   *Lupinus aridus*

Sulphur lupine   *Lupinus sulphureus*

Foothills lupine   *Lupinus ammophilus*

Sweetvetch   *Hedysarum boreale*

Sweetvetch, also called northern hedysarum, closely resembles some of the larger locoweeds (*Astragalus* species) and occupies similar habitats. It differs, however, in having red or purplish-red flowers—an unusual color among locoweeds—and flattened pods with obvious constrictions between the seeds. The plants present a bushy appearance with their numerous one- to two-feet-tall branched stems. The leaves are pinnately compound with seven to fifteen oval leaflets. The reddish flowers, bilaterally symmetrical and pea-like, form congested, elongate, showy racemes. The generic name, of Greek derivation (*hedy* means sweet, *sarum* means broom), probably relates to the pleasant fragrance of the flowers and broom-like aspect of the erect, many-stemmed plants.

Sweetvetch ranges from the Canadian arctic tundra into the southern Rockies. It is fairly common in the high plains, especially in the Rocky Mountain region, where it grows in fine-textured, often clayey soils. It flowers in early summer or late spring. Unlike locoweed and crazyweed, this species is not poisonous and, in fact, historically was collected and eaten by Indians. The roots especially are tasty (licorice-like) and nutritious.

Steppe sweetpea   *Lathyrus pauciflorus*

This is the only species of wild sweetpeas (*Lathyrus* species) that prefers the steppe to other habitats. A low, weak-stemmed perennial, steppe sweetpea produces one or a few flowering stalks per plant. The showy sweetpea-like flowers are lavender-purple in short racemes. As the specific epithet suggests, there are only a few (four to eight) flowers per raceme (*pauci* means few, *florus* means flower). The three to five terminal leaflets of the pinnately compound leaves are modified into tendrils, which the plants use to attach to and climb associated plants, such as sagebrush. The possession of tendrils, along with the sweetpea-like flowers, clearly distinguish this species from other legumes of the sagebrush steppe.

Steppe sweetpea grows more or less throughout the sagebrush steppe, though seldom in abundance. It lives primarily in the upper, more moist areas, extending upward into ponderosa pine forests and piñon-juniper woodlands. Steppe sweetpea flowers early in the spring and provides a very important food source for queen bumblebees emerging from winter hibernation.

Sweetvetch   *Hedysarum boreale*

Sweetvetch   *Hedysarum boreale*

Steppe sweetpea   *Lathyrus pauciflorus*

107

Golden pea   *Thermopsis montana*

The showy, golden-yellow flowers and the graceful, three-foliate leaves—with leafy appendages at the base of the leaf stalks—combine to make the golden pea a very attractive plant. The coarse stems reach nearly three feet tall and bear several leaves. The pea-like flowers are borne in a somewhat elongate but usually dense raceme. Silky hair usually covers the sepals, the upper part of the stem, and the narrow, erect pods.

The golden pea rather closely resembles lupine in many respects; the name *Thermopsis* comes from the Greek *thermos* meaning lupine and *opsis* meaning resemblance. However, none of the lupines has such bright yellow flowers, and all have more than three leaflets. The golden pea most frequently lives in meadows where it often forms dense populations, partly as a result of its unpalatability. Occasionally it grows in the moister areas of the high plains, often associated with sagebrush. The golden pea is widespread in western North America, from the western steppelands into Colorado.

Large-headed clover   *Trifolium macrocephalum*

Large-headed clover is unusual in a number of respects. While most clovers grow in moist soils or as weeds in disturbed areas, this species is certainly not weedy and grows only in thin, rocky (lithosol) areas that become very dry during the hot summer. Clovers characteristically have three ("tri") leaflets ("folium"), but the large-headed clover has five or six, and in this respect the leaves resemble those of lupines.

The large-headed clover is also our most attractive species of *Trifolium*. This sprawling, hairy plant spreads by rootstalks, called rhizomes, and forms dense and often extensive populations. The pink to lavender or orchid, pea-like flowers cluster densely in showy heads one and one half to two inches in diameter. A regular member of lithosol communities in eastern Washington and adjacent Oregon and Idaho, large-headed clover extends southward into Nevada and upward into similar habitats in ponderosa pine forests. It flowers in early spring.

Golden pea *Thermopsis montana*

Prairie lupine *Lupinus*

Large-headed clover *Trifolium macrocephalum*

PHLOX FAMILY Polemoniaceae

This is a large family characterized by its stereotypic butterfly/moth flowers. The petals fuse into a long, narrow tube with five spreading lobes. Only a long-tongued insect can reach the nectar concealed at the base of the floral tube. The stamens, or filaments, are fused to the floral tube, and the ovary contains three styles, an important family characteristic.

Large-flowered collomia *Collomia grandiflora*

Large-flowered collomia produces very attractive flowers of an unusual pale salmon color. The plant is a tall annual (up to three feet) with a single stem that often branches along the upper half. The leaves are two to four inches long, lance-shaped or elliptical, and borne uniformly along the stem. The flowers form a showy round-topped head. Each flower has five sepals and five petals, the latter fused into a long and very narrow, nectar-containing tube with perpendicular lobes. The dark-colored stamens lie near the throat of the floral tube.

Large-flowered collomia appears sporadically in dry, sandy habitats over a broad geographical range west of the Continental Divide. It flowers in late spring.

A much smaller, related plant is **narrow-leafed collomia (*Collomia linearis*)**, an extremely common but rather inconspicuous, branched annual. Its stems vary in height depending on soil conditions, but rarely reach more than one foot tall. The leaves, narrowly lance-shaped, are borne along the full length of the stem. The small tubular flowers vary in color from the usual pink or pale lavender to white and develop in heads at the ends of branches. This early flowering, small annual inhabits high plains and open mountain ridges throughout the steppe.

Large-flowered collomia *Collomia grandiflora*

Large-flowered collomia *Collomia grandiflora*
Narrow-leafed collomia *Collomia linearis*

Phlox

Phlox is a Greek word meaning flame, a fitting name for this group of plants with their condensed mass of brilliant color. The predominant flower color is pink but may vary to blue, lilac-purple, or even white. The stems, usually extensively branched, present a low, cushion-like profile. Some plants become somewhat shrubby at the base. The leaves are numerous, opposite at the condensed nodes, narrow, and often sharp-pointed. The petals fuse to form a "trumpet" with a long, narrow tube and five flaring lobes. Neither the stamens nor the style extends beyond the floral tube.

As a group, the phloxes are among the most desirable rock garden wildflowers, combining beauty with the ability to grow in dry climates.

Among the many species, **long-leaf phlox** (*Phlox longifolia*) is the most common and widespread, growing more or less throughout the high plains of the sagebrush steppe. This rather weak-stemmed, pink-flowered plant frequently reaches through and clambers over the branches of sagebrush and other steppe shrubs. It has linear and, as the common name suggests, relatively long (one to three inch) leaves.

Showy phlox (*Phlox speciosa*) resembles long-leaf phlox but differs in having heart-shaped petal lobes. This rather tall plant often clambers over steppe shrubs, creating a beautiful display. The flowers are pink or white, with green striped sepals. The leaves are lance-shaped. Glandular-sticky, strong-smelling hair covers the sepals. Showy phlox has a rather restricted range, inhabiting only the northern and western part of the sagebrush steppe.

A very common low, compact plant is **cushion phlox** (*Phlox hoodii*), which grows throughout the sagebrush steppe, mostly in dry, rocky (lithosol) habitats. Its showy flowers vary in color from purple to shades of blue, red, or occasionally white. The leaves are linear but stiff and spiny. It flowers very early in the spring.

A similar but less compact, white-flowered, cushion species from Idaho and Montana is multiflowered phlox (*Phlox multiflora*). It extends from the high steppes onto rocky ridges.

Long-leafed plox   *Plox longifolia*   **Showy phlox**   *Phlox speciosa*

Cushion phlox   *Phlox hoodii*

Granite gilia

Leptodactylon pungens

If the flowering plants of the steppe were ranked on the basis of overall attractiveness, granite gilia would not fare well. It is a low spreading, rather ragged-looking shrub with many small, spine-tipped leaves that cluster at the nodes. (In Greek, *Lepto* means fine, *dactylo* means finger; in Latin *pungens* means spine-like.) Dead leaves often remain on the branches, becoming unsightly and rigidly spiny. The white to salmon-colored flowers are not unattractive but are seldom seen fully open. They open at night to be pollinated by nocturnal moths. During the day they close or partially close in a twisting pattern. When open they create a long, narrow tube with five spreading petal lobes and cluster loosely near the ends of the leafy branches.

Granite gilia is widely distributed in the steppes and deserts of North America, usually inhabiting rocky, lithosol and coarse talus or granitic slopes. It flowers very early in the spring.

Scarlet gilia

Gilia aggregata

Scarlet gilia is a conspicuous plant with strikingly attractive, trumpet-shaped flowers that vary in color from typically brilliant scarlet, speckled with white, to pale pink or yellowish speckled with red. The lighter-colored forms are more common in Nevada, Utah, and southern Wyoming and are pollinated by hawk moths. The typical scarlet form grows throughout the sagebrush steppe, extending upward into piñon-juniper woodlands and open ponderosa pine forests and onto mountain ridges. It is pollinated primarily by hummingbirds.

Stems of the scarlet gilia reach up to three feet tall, are often branched, and have several flowers. They arise from an elongate, carrot-like taproot. Most of the attractively divided leaves appear at the base of the stem. Often the stems and leaves are glandular-sticky and fragrant.

Scarlet gilia is a biennial. The first year each plant consists of a clump of divided leaves that produce an abundance of food to be stored in the enlarged taproot. The second year the plant uses the stored food to very rapidly grow and reproduce before dying. The abundant stored food enables the plants to tolerate and even benefit from grazing with increased branching and greater production of flowers and seeds.

Granite gilia *Leptodactylon pungens*

Scarlet gilia *Gilia aggregata*

Scarlet gilia *Gilia aggregata*

115

PINK FAMILY   Caryophyllaceae

Although this is a large and diverse family, a combination of traits set it apart from other families. Plants are herbaceous with opposite leaves borne from enlarged (swollen) nodes. The ovary matures into a capsule-shaped fruit with numerous seeds produced along a central column. The flowers are radially symmetrical, usually with five petals and ten stamens. Most species of the pink family grow in moist, cool habitats, such as the alpine zone. Some, including sandworts, inhabit both high mountains and sagebrush plains.

Sandworts   *Arenaria* species

The sandworts are cushion plants with very narrow, sometimes spiny, leaves. The generic name comes from the Latin *arena*, which means sand, the characteristic habitat of most sandworts. (Wort is an old English word for plant.) Four rather common species inhabit the sagebrush steppe.

Franklin's sandwort   *Arenaria franklinii*

Franklin's sandwort is a distinctive plant that forms very dense cushions several inches in diameter. The plant produces two types of tightly packed stems: (1) non-flowering stems, which are never more than one or two inches tall, and have numerous, opposite, linear and sharply pointed leaves; and (2) flowering stems, which are somewhat taller, have fewer leaves, and produce several flowers in compact clusters. The rather showy flowers bear sharply pointed, green-ribbed sepals and somewhat longer (1/3 inch long), white petals. Franklin's sandwort commonly grows in sandy soils, often in dunes, west of the Rocky Mountains.

A very similar species is desert sandwort (*Arenaria hookeri*), found in sandy or gravelly soil in dry sagebrush plains in the Rocky Mountain region, mostly east of the Continental Divide.

Prickly sandwort   *Arenaria aculeata*

As the common name suggests, the leaves of prickly sandwort are stiff and sharply pointed. Most are basal, the ones on the stem smaller in size. Each flowering stem bears three to five flowers about one half inch across. Prickly sandwort grows in the southern portion of the sagebrush steppe, from northeastern California to Utah. It is equally at home in gravelly sagebrush hills and rocky alpine slopes.

Mountain sandwort   *Arenaria capillaris*

As is true of the prickly sandwort, mountain sandwort covers a broad elevational range, from sagebrush plains to subalpine slopes. The leaves grow primarily at the base of the plant but often surpass the flowering stems in length. They are rather stiff, but not sharp-pointed, and very narrow, thread-like. The white flowers are about one half inch across, with one or only a few per flower stem. Mountain sandwort ranges from Washington to Montana, south into Oregon and Nevada.

Franklin's sandwort *Arenaria franklinii*

Prickly sandwort *Arenaria aculeata*
Mountain sandwort *Arenaria capillaris*

PLANTAIN FAMILY   Plantaginceaae

This small family is represented by a single native species in the sagebrush steppe: **hairy plantain (*Plantago patagonica*)**, a small woolly annual less than six inches tall. The narrow leaves all unfurl at the base of the plant, leaving the stems leafless. Although the flowers are by no means showy, this plant derives a certain attractiveness from its long woolly hairs and white, widely-spreading, papery petals nestled among the hair of the spike. Interestingly, this and other species of *Plantago* exemplify an intermediate stage between an insect-pollinated plant, with showy flowers, and a wind-pollinated plant, with reduced non-functional petals, long stamens that extend beyond the confines of the flower, and feathery stigmas that comb the air for pollen.

Hairy plantain inhabits the western part of the sagebrush steppe, from British Columbia to California, growing mostly in dry, sandy soils or mildly alkaline sites. It frequently invades disturbed areas, especially those subjected to overgrazing, which tends to eliminate the more competitive grasses.

POPPY FAMILY   Papaveraceae

Although several species of poppies inhabit the American deserts, few extend north into the sagebrush steppe. The family is characterized in part by having four or six petals and numerous stamens.

Prickly poppy   *Argemone platyceras*

The leaves and stems of the prickly poppy resemble those of thistles, but the flowers and fruit differ greatly. Needle-sharp spines and prickles cover the coarse and branched stems. The leaves are variously lobed and clasp the stem, with spines along the margins and midvein. The showy flowers project from branch tips among the leaves, and each has numerous stamens, three spiny green sepals, and six delicate white, two- to three-inch petals. The fruit, typical of poppies, has a round base and flattened cap with scalloped edges and small pores that allow the seeds to escape when shaken by the wind.

The conspicuous and well-marked prickly poppy grows in somewhat sandy and gravelly habitats of the Great Basin, extending southward into the deserts. Like most poppies, it contains alkaloids known to be toxic to man and other animals. The plants are rarely eaten, however, either because of their spininess, distastefulness, or both.

Hairy plantain *Plantago patigonica*

Prickly poppy *Argemone platyceras*

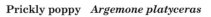

Prickly poppy *Argemone platyceras*

PRIMROSE FAMILY   Primulaceae

Primulaceae is a small family with only one genus, *Dodecatheon*, regularly inhabiting the steppeland. Therefore, the characteristics of the family, which are largely technical in any case, prove of little relevance.

Shooting star   *Dodecatheon* species

Although the various species of shooting star love moisture and therefore grow primarily in moist or marshy meadows, some occasionally inhabit the plains and foothills of sagebrush communities. Even here, they grow in flat areas of poor drainage, where moisture persists late into the season, and in ravines that carry runoff from melting snow. The plants complete their reproductive cycle very quickly while the soil is moist.

The attractive shooting stars are easily identified by their elliptical, somewhat strap-like, non-toothed leaves (all basal) in combination with their unique flowers. These consist of five sepals and five petals reflexed backward away from the colorful stamens, which more or less fuse into a tube surrounding the style. The total effect of the nodding, purplish-lavender or white flower is that of a shooting star. Even in the days of Greek mythology, this genus gained respect for its beauty and unusual appearance as attested to by its name: *dodeca* (twelve), *theon* (gods). As the story goes, the twelve gods assumed the responsibility of watching over some member or members of this genus.

The unusual shape of the shooting star flower reveals biological significance. The flower has adapted to be "buzz" pollinated by bumblebees. These clever insects grasp the base of the stamens, marked by a bright yellow band, hang upside down, and vibrate, or buzz, the flowers. In this way the pollen shakes out of the tube of anthers onto the abdomen of the bee. The bee then combs the pollen into sacs to carry it back to the hive. Some of the pollen remains on the bee, and when she visits another flower, the elongated style positions the stigma precisely where the residual pollen is located. The flowers get pollinated, the bees get food for the larvae.

The two most common shooting stars within the sagebrush steppe are **Dodecatheon pulchellum** and **Dodecatheon conjugens**. The former is more widespread and common, but both grow more or less throughout the steppe. In suitable habitats they occasionally form very large and spectacular populations.

Shooting star
Dodecatheon pulchellum

Shooting star
Dodecatheon conjugens

Shooting star   *Dodecatheon pulchellum*

PURSLANE FAMILY   Portulacaceae

A combination of rather technical characteristics unifies the purslane family. However, the flowers of most species have only two sepals in combination with five petals and five stamens. Bitterroot is an exception to this generality. All family members are more or less succulent.

Spring beauty   *Claytonia lanceolata*

Although the spring beauty seems more at home in mountain meadows and on alpine slopes, it is not uncommon in the high sagebrush plains. Here it grows in areas of abundant spring moisture, usually where run-off collects from melting snow fields. It often forms very dense populations, flowering within a few days of snow recession; it is indeed a "spring beauty."

The plants are mostly less than six inches high, with deeply buried bulbs from which a few to several weak, succulent, brittle stems are derived, each bearing a pair of strongly veined, lance-shaped leaves. The flowers develop in an elongate cluster, or raceme, above the two leaves. Each flower has two green sepals, five white to pink (with darker stripes), notched petals, and five stamens. The starchy and potato-like bulbs reputedly have toxic properties unless cooked. Still, they have been widely gathered in the past as a food source. Spring beauty grows throughout the higher altitudes and latitudes of the sagebrush steppe.

Bitterroot   *Lewisia rediviva*

The unusual bitterroot, or rock rose, grows along rocky ridges and in thin soils of basalt flats, where it remains inconspicuous among the rocks or in the rocky crevices until the beautiful and delicate flowers appear. Each flower has numerous petals, stamens, and styles, and in this respect the bitterroot resembles a cactus. The petals, approximately one inch long, vary in color from nearly white to deep rose and often display darker longitudinal stripes. The succulent leaves are small (one to three inches long), club-shaped, and inconspicuous. All are borne at ground level or below from carrot-like roots. The fleshiness of the bitterroot reflects a water storing adaptation, which parallels that of cacti and other "desert" succulents. The roots can survive extreme dehydration, an ability reflected in the name "rediviva."

In the past, Plains Indians dug the plants and then peeled and boiled the roots before eating them. The plants were collected early in the spring because as the plants age the roots become woody and bitter. Lewis and Clark also collected this species along what is now known as the Bitterroot River in Montana. The genus honorably bears the name of Captain Meriwether Lewis.

The attractive bitterroot, the state flower of Montana, is widely distributed in the sagebrush steppe and along adjacent montane ridges. It flowers in early summer, after most of its lithosol associates.

Spring beauty   *Claytonia lanceolata*   **Spring beauty   *Claytonia lanceolata***

Bitterroot   *Lewisia rediviva*

ROSE FAMILY
Rosaceae

The flowers of the rose family resemble those of the buttercup family except that the sepals fuse at the base to form a tube or a saucer upon which the petals and stamens lie. The flowers of the rose family also have numerous stamens and two to several pistils. The family varies greatly and includes plants of all forms, from small annuals to large trees.

Old man's beard
Geum triflorum

Although somewhat inconspicuous in its habitat, old man's beard is nevertheless an unusual and attractive plant. The basal fern-like leaves are pinnately compound with deeply toothed leaflets that get progressively larger toward the leaf tip. The flowering stems remain leafless, with the exception of two, small dissected leaves near midlength. The flowers normally come in threes (as the species name implies), associated with dissected leaf-like bracts. The reddish sepals fuse at the base to form a bowl-shaped structure from which the five petals and numerous stamens arise. The yellow to red petals are nearly hidden by the sepals. Long, soft hairs sparsely to densely cover the entire plant. As the fruits, or achenes, mature, the styles become very long and feathery, collectively presenting the appearance of a long, white beard. The feathery styles aid in wind dispersal of the single-seeded achenes. The roots have an interesting sassafras-like taste and can be boiled to make a refreshing tea.

This species grows in the more moist sites of the steppeland, particularly the high plains of the Rockies. It ranges from Canada to Nevada, Arizona, and New Mexico.

Cinquefoil
Potentilla species

Potentilla forms a complex genus of several species with buttercup-like flowers. The leaves vary from strawberry-like, or ternate, to pinnately or palmately compound. The common name relates to species posessing palmate leaves with five leaflets. The flowers are usually bright yellow, but pale yellow to almost white varieties exist. Most species inhabit open forests and/or subalpine meadows; a few grow in the steppelands. Among the latter group, **slender cinquefoil (*Potentilla gracilis*)** is the most widespread. Usually one to two feet tall, it produces several stems and numerous palmately compound leaves, the basal ones having long slender leaf stalks. The common name does not strictly apply since the leaves have six to nine leaflets, rather than five. The dense foliage is very attractive with deeply toothed leaflets and silky-gray pubescence. Showy, bright yellow flowers form a branched, flat-topped display above the leaves. Each flower has five sepals and five lower bracts, five petals, and numerous stamens and small ovaries. Slender cinquefoil grows most commonly in the high plains and mountains where sagebrush communities overlap with open forests. It also extends upward along montane ridges into subalpine meadows and ranges throughout western North America. It flowers in early summer.

Old man's beard (*Geum triflorum*) flowers

Old man's beard (*Geum triflorum*) fruit

Slender cinquefoil   *Potentilla gracilis*

Bitterbrush   *Purshia tridentata*

Bitterbrush, also called antelope bush, often dominates communities immediately below ponderosa pine forests and piñon-juniper woodlands. It also commonly grows on dry, open, south-facing slopes of mountain ridges. In general, it prefers sandy or rocky, well-drained soils in habitats somewhat more moist than is typical for the sagebrush steppe. Bitterbrush is usually associated with balsamroots (*Balsamorhiza*) or mules ears (*Wyethia*). This medium-sized, extensively branched shrub produces many small three-lobed leaves similar to those of sagebrush, but because they lack the gray, woolly hair, are brighter green or sometimes olive-green. The flowers are small but bright yellow and abundant, making the shrubs attractive during the flowering period in late spring. Although it tastes bitter, this shrub provides an extremely important food source for deer, especially in the winter on windswept, relatively snow-free slopes. Here, the plants often become stunted from excessive browsing.

Bitterbrush ranges from Washington and Oregon eastward through Wyoming, north into Canada, and south into Utah, Colorado, Nevada, and California. In the southern extreme of its range, it overlaps and hybridizes with the closely related cliffrose (*Cowania stransburiana*).

Serviceberry   *Amelanchier alnifolia*

Serviceberry is widely distributed over western North America, and although most common in open forests, it frequently grows in coarse talus and other rocky slopes of the sagebrush steppe, particularly along canyon walls. It also commonly inhabits aspen groves which themselves exist as "island" communities in the upper sagebrush steppe.

Serviceberry, a large, variable-sized shrub, bears many attractive and fragrant white spring flowers, each with rather narrow and elongate petals and numerous stamens. The ovate to elliptical leaves are toothed toward the tip. The juicy and tasty fruit turns bluish-purple when ripe, resembles a miniature apple, and makes good jelly, and pie. The berries provide a staple food source for birds and other animals, and the species is valuable as a browse plant for wildlife, particularly deer.

Bitterbrush   *Purshia tridentata*

Bitterbrush community with lupine

Serviceberry   *Amelanchier alnifolia*

SANDALWOOD FAMILY   Santalaceae

Only one sandalwood species inhabits the sagebrush steppe: **bastard toad-flax** (*Comandra umbellata*). As its common name implies, this plant is rather unattractive. It seldom reaches more than twelve inches tall, the erect stems growing in clumps from spreading root-stalks called rhizomes. Each stem produces numerous alternate, elliptical gray-green leaves. The flowers form a terminal flat-topped or rounded cluster. Petals are absent and the sepals vary in color from green to pale purplish. The ovary is inferior (borne below the sepals and stamens) and matures into a berry-like, blue, purplish, or brown fruit. The fruit, though normally edible, may contain deleterious amounts of selenium which the plants accumulate if growing in selenium-rich soils.

Like several unrelated plants of the steppe, bastard toad-flax is a root parasite, extracting materials from a wide range of host plants. Although fully photosynthetic and apparently able to survive without a host, this plant enjoys an extremely wide range undoubtedly in part because of its parasite-host relationship. Bastard toad-flax grows throughout the semi-arid region of western North America, becoming especially abundant in moderately sandy soils.

Bastard toad-flax   *Comandra umbellata*

SAXIFRAGE FAMILY   Saxifragaceae

The steppe species of the saxifrage family are all perennial herbs with mostly basal leaves that are usually palmately lobed or divided. The flowers vary but usually have five petals, five sepals and ten stamens. The sepals are fused into a short tube or a saucer.

Prairie star flower   *Lithophragma* species

The prairie star flowers stand out with their unusual blossoms and attractive leaves. The white to pinkish petals are deeply lobed from the tip into three narrow segments. The flowers develop in a short raceme near the stem tip. The leaves are palmately lobed or divided, the basal ones being larger and stalked. The weak stems grow not more than one foot tall.

Two species of *Lithophragma* live more or less throughout the sagebrush steppe. The smaller-flowered of these, **Lithophragma bulbifera**, gets its name from the reddish bulblets borne in the angle where the reduced upper stem leaves meet the stem. The sepals and stems are typically dark red. The second common species, **Lithophragma parviflora**, lacks the bulblets on the stem noted above and has lighter colored stems and sepals. It also produces larger flowers, even though *parviflora* means small flower. Both species have fibrous roots with associated small bulblets. These bulblets may produce toxins that lead to livestock poisoning when animals pull up the plants by the roots during wet spring weather. However, rodents eat the bulblets without apparent harm.

Prairie star flowers extend from dry sagebrush communities to meadows, grassy hillsides, open forests, and rocky ridges. They are among the first plants to flower in the spring.

Alumroot   *Heuchera cylindrica*

Although the flowers of alumroot are not particularly showy, the plants add beauty to their rocky setting with their numerous dark green, palmately lobed, basal leaves with long leaf stalks. The straight, leafless stems reach up to three feet tall with a dense terminal spike of cream-colored to greenish-yellow flowers. The petals are small and inconspicuous or absent, and the sepals fuse at the base to form a cup with five lobes. Short, straight hairs usually cover the plants.

This alumroot is the most widespread and probably most drought tolerant of several closely related species of *Heuchera*. It grows on rock ledges and talus slopes in the high plains and mountains of western North America. Easily transplanted or grown from seed, it contributes nicely to the native rock garden.

Prairie star flower
Lithophragma bulbifera

Prairie star flower
Lithophragma parviflora

Alumroot *Heuchera cylindrica*

STONECROP FAMILY   Crassulaceae

A single genus, *Sedum*, represents this family in the sagebrush steppe. The common name for the genus and family derives from the typical stony habitat of the various species. The plants have adapted to tolerate a lack of soil and exposure to the wind and sun by storing and conserving water in the succulent stems and leaves. The plants typically form mats that spread by short runners or rootstalks, called rhizomes. Stems are usually of two types: erect stems that produce flowers and dwarf stems that bear bundles of leaves. Most species produce bright yellow, star-shaped flowers with five, sharp-pointed petals and ten stamens. Each flower has five ovaries that mature into pod-like fruits called follicles that split open at maturity to disseminate the seeds.

The two most common steppe species are **lance-leaf stonecrop (*Sedum lanceolatum*)** and **worm-leaf stonecrop (*Sedum stenopetalum*)**. Lance-leaf stonecrop has erect flowering stems (four to six inches tall). The sharp-pointed and lance-shaped leaves are nearly round in cross section and about one half inch long. The five many-seeded fruits stand more or less erect at maturity, and the bright yellow flowers form a rather dense, branched cluster at the stem tips. Worm-leaf stonecrop has thinner and less strictly erect flowering stems. The leaves are longer and narrower, often crooked (worm-like), and sharply pointed. Flowers cluster less densely, and the fruits spread outward, star-like, at maturity.

Both species are widely distributed in the sagebrush steppe, growing on rock outcrops and lithosols and extending their range upward into similar rocky habitats of the alpine zone. Both flower in the summer rather than spring.

Lance-leaf stonecrop   *Sedum lanceolatum*

Lance-leaf stonecrop   *Sedum lanceolatum*
Worm-leaf stonecrop   *Sedum stenopetalum*

SUNFLOWER (or Aster) FAMILY Compositae

This is the largest family of flowering plants in the world, the largest in North America, and the largest in the sagebrush steppe. Although they vary widely, the family's numerous species clearly reveal their relationship through the flower and inflorescence characteristics. Flowers develop in a head, or composite, surrounded by involucral bracts of variable size, shape, and color, depending on species. The flowers are of two types, disk and ray, which may occur in combination or apart, again depending on species. When both flower types exist, ray flowers are on the outside, each resembling a single petal, immediately inside the involucral bracts. In disk flowers, the five petals are fused together into a tumpet-shaped tube with five short petal lobes. In ray flowers, the petals are all fused into a strap-like appendage that resembles a single petal. The five anthers are also fused along their edges to form a tube through which the style grows, pushing out the pollen and presenting it to pollinators. The highly modified sepals, collectively termed the pappus, usually take the form of numerous bristles. For a better understanding of floral characteristics, see the illustrations.

The sunflower family, very important ecologically, includes many of the dominant steppe species, even sagebrush itself. Most species have conspicuous, brightly colored heads of insect-pollinated flowers; others, such as sagebrush, produce small heads with minute flowers that are wind pollinated. Species vary in habit from diminutive annuals to large shrubs.

Aster
Aster species

As a group, asters are distinguished by a combination of relatively few blue, pink, or white rays (usually with fewer than 25 per head), leafy, branched stems with several heads, and a flowering period of mid- to late summer. With some exceptions, including the three described below, the asters of the steppe are weedy roadside species.

Rocky Mountain aster (*Aster adscendens*) is perhaps the most common aster of the Rocky Mountain and Great Basin area. It closely resembles and is often mistaken for the smaller-flowered *A chilensis*. This typical erect aster produces numerous heads per stem. The pale blue to lavender rays are about one half inch long.

Woody-rooted aster (*Aster xylorrhiza*) is a daisy-like cushion plant with many, mostly basal leaves and large heads with white rays. It inhabits somewhat moist lowland sites in the plains of the Great Basin and flowers in early summer.

Lava aster (*Aster scopulorum*) is also a low daisy-like plant with few to several stems, each bearing a single head. The blue-violet rays, usually eight in number, are approximately one half inch long. The narrowly elliptical leaves, also about one half inch long, crowd along the middle of the stem. The lava aster grows in dry, rocky (lithosol) sites in northern Nevada and parts of Idaho and Oregon. It flowers in early summer.

Rocky Moutnain aster *Aster adscendens*

Woody-rooted aster *Aster xylorrhiza*
Lava aster *Aster scopulorum*

Daisy   *Erigeron* species

The many colorful daisies constitute an ecologically important and conspicuous element of the steppe vegetation. Most species have the typical daisy-like flower consisting of showy heads with inner, usually yellow, disk flowers and numerous narrow blue, pink to purple, or occasionally white or yellow outer rays. Rarely the rays are absent. Most daisies have several short and erect flowering stems, each bearing a single head. The many narrow, elongate leaves cluster predominantly near the base of the stems, giving the plants a cushion-like appearance. The steppe daisies flower in spring or early summer.

Several genera of the sagebrush steppe appear very similar, distinguishable largely by technical characteristics. Many of these genera are routinely referred to as daisies, including species of *Aster* and *Townsendia*. In general, *Erigeron* can be separated from *Aster* by growth form (asters are generally more erect with few, leafy stems), time of flowering (asters usually flower in midsummer rather than early spring), and number of ray flowers (asters usually have fewer than 25). *Townsendia* is more difficult to distinguish from *Erigeron*, and such distinction can be done only by comparing the pappus: *Townsendia* has a scale-like pappus while *Erigeron* has numerous capillary bristles. *Erigeron* is a much larger genus.

Although many of the daisies cover a broad ecological range, the arrangement here loosely groups them according to habitat.

Daisies of sandy soils

Only a few daisies seem to prefer sandy soils. Among these, the most common is probably the **thread-leafed daisy (*Erigeron filifolius*)**, whose name comes from its linear leaves. The plants branch extensively from the base, forming rather large, symmetrical clumps. The individual stems also branch, producing a few to several flower heads with pale blue to pink or, more frequently, white rays. This species is widely distributed from British Columbia south to California and east across Nevada to the plains of Wyoming.

A highly variable but distinctive daisy of sandy to gravelly soils is **shaggy daisy (*Erigeron pumilus*)**. This species grows more erect than most daisies but still has several flowering stems. The heads are rather small with several white or occasionally pale pink or blue rays. Also distinctive are the characteristically dense and stiff hairs that give the entire plant a shaggy appearance, hence, the common name. This species grows throughout the steppeland but is seldom common.

A Great Basin daisy that extends southward into the deserts is **Basin rayless daisy (*Erigeron aphanactis*)**. As the common name indicates, this species lacks rays but has rather large heads with attractive bright yellow disk flowers. The absence of rays, unusual among daisies, distinguishes this species. This is perhaps the most drought tolerant of the steppe daisies. It grows in sandy or rocky sites.

Thread-leafed daisy *Erigeron filifolius*

Shaggy daisy *Erigeron pumilus*
Basin rayless daisy *Erigeron aphanactis*

Daisies of lithosols and talus

Lithosols often provide beautiful displays of wildflowers in early spring, truly the rock gardens of the sagebrush steppe. The plants have adapted to complete their growth and reproduction quickly before entering into a long period of dormancy. By late spring, lithosol areas appear lifeless except for a few hardy species such as stiff sagebrush and desert buckwheats. Some of the more colorful components of the lithosol gardens are daisies.

Among the species that form brilliant displays is **linear-leaf daisy** (*Erigeron linearis*). This dense cushion plant produces narrow basal leaves and numerous short upright flowering stems, each with a single head. Linear-leaf daisy is unusual, but not unique, in having yellow rays. It thrives in the western "half" of the sagebrush steppe, especially in the basaltic areas of the Columbia basin.

Within the steppelands of Wyoming, Colorado, and Utah, one of the most common daisies is the low, white-flowered **plains daisy (*Erigeron engelmannii*)**. While certainly not restricted to lithosols or talus slopes this daisy grows most prevalently in dry, thin rocky or gravelly soils. The narrow leaves widen toward the tip. They are borne on the stem as well as at the base of the small cushion plants. The small flower heads, usually less than an inch across, produce many white rays and yellow to orange disk flowers.

A showy daisy of rocky or sandy habitats in eastern Washington, Oregon, and western Idaho is **cushion daisy (*Erigeron poliospermus*)**. This low, few-stemmed species yields colorful purple to pale violet, inch-long rays. The narrow leaves, mostly basal, are covered with short, stiff hairs.

Linear-leaf daisy *Erigeron linearis*

Plains daisy *Erigeron engelmannii*

Cushion daisy *Erigeron poliospermus*

Steppe communities, including those dominated by sagebrush, extend upward along south-facing slopes into the subalpine zone. On these high mountain ridges, daisies (*Erigeron* and *Townsendia*) are well represented. With the exception of cooler nights and harsher winters, the environment here resembles that of the plains below, as does the vegetation. The daisies found along these ridges typically grow low and cushion-like. The stems and leaves are usually densely covered with hairs that protect them from water loss in summer heat and nearly incessant wind.

A very common daisy on rocky mountain ridges, but also extending down onto the high plains, is **dwarf mountain daisy (*Erigeron compositus*)**. This low, hairy plant has short stems rising from a dense cushion of basal leaves. Each stem bears a single head of showy pale blue to lavender rays. Unlike those of most other daisies the leaves are divided at the tip.

Rough daisy (*Erigeron asperugineus*) is one of the most colorful of the mountain species. The usually solitary flower heads bloom on nearly leafless, lax stems that spread and tend to lie on the ground. The rays are one half inch long and unusually dark (lavender-purple) for daisies. The basal leaves have wavy margins and widen gradually toward the tip. The common name describes the short, dense hair that covers the leaves. Rough daisy grows commonly in the central Rocky Mountain region (Idaho, Utah, and Nevada).

Townsendia or daisy   *Townsendia* species

The similarities between species of *Townsendia* and those of *Erigeron* (both daisies) are much more impressive than are the differences. It is extremely difficult to distinguish between the two genera without reference to technical characteristics. However, the townsendias usually have larger heads and shorter flowering stalks. As is typical of most daisies, plants have both disk and ray flowers, the latter colorful and attractive.

Probably the most common steppe species is **Parry's daisy (*Townsendia parryi*)**, which extends upward onto rocky ridges. This short-lived plant rises from a taproot. Very short stems bear single, large heads as much as two inches across. The flowers appear to be lying on the ground among the sparse leaves that broaden toward the tip. The rays, pale lavender to blue, are long and attractive. This species grows throughout the Rocky Mountains and adjacent plains. It is particularly common in southwest Montana.

An attractive, smaller version of Parry's daisy is **showy townsendia (*Townsendia florifer*)**. This species bears single heads of pastel lavender flowers on short, clustered flowering stems. Showy townsendia is a rather common plant of the sagebrush steppe.

Dwarf mountain daisy *Erigeron compositus*

Rough daisy *Erigeron asperugineus*
Parry's daisy *Townsendia parryi*

Goldenweed   *Haplopappus* species

Haplopappus is a large and variable genus including both shrubs and herbs. The heads produce both ray and disk flowers, both golden yellow. The species closely resemble daisies (*Erigeron*) but can be easily distinguished by having fewer rays, usually about ten. Also, the goldenweeds grow abundantly in the desert regions of North America, whereas the daisies grow primarily in the steppe.

Dwarf goldenweed (*Haplopappus acaulis*) is an attractive woody-based cushion plant with a stout taproot and branched root crown. The roots give rise to several short and erect, nearly leafless stems, each bearing a single showy head. The leaves, small and narrow (mostly less than two inches long) and rigidly erect, crowd the base of the plant. The yellow heads have approximately eight to ten colorful rays and several disk flowers. Dwarf goldenweed is common and widespread in the steppe, absent only from Washington where it is replaced by *Haplopappus stenophyllus*, a species that grows in very dry, rocky sites on the plains and along open ridges.

The very attractive **thrift goldenweed (*Haplopappus armerioid*)** resembles dwarf goldenweed but is larger in all aspects. The two closely related species overlap in distribution but thrift goldenweed is more common east of the Rocky Mountains and south in the Great Basin. They both require dry, rocky or gravelly soils.

A low, unattractive, ragged-looking shrub, **matchbrush (*Gutierrezia sarothrae)*** is nevertheless conspicuous because it often forms dense populations and because it flowers during late summer after most steppe species have become dormant. The brittle, extensively branched plants seldom grow more than a foot tall and bear many very narrow (linear) leaves, usually slightly more than one inch long. The lower leaves soon dry and fall off. Both the ray and disk flowers are yellow, few in number (three to seven), and borne in small heads which themselves branch in terminal clusters.

Under natural conditions, matchbrush tends to grow only in nonproductive rocky habitats of dry sagebrush plains; however, with overgrazing it invades better soils. When food is scarce, livestock feed on matchbrush, which causes various and multiple intestinal disorders, abortion, weak offspring, and occasionally death. The species is common in the eastern "half" of the steppe, barely reaching into Washington and Oregon.

Dwarf goldenweed *Haplopappus acaulis*

Thrift goldenweed *Haplopappus armerioides*
Matchbrush *Gutierrezia sarothrae*

Rabbit-brush   *Chrysothamnus* species

An extremely common steppe shrub, rabbit-brush rivals sagebrush in its distribution and ecological importance. Frequently they share habitats as codominants of steppe communities; occasionally rabbit-brush forms rather pure stands. However, it has a more restricted ecological range than sagebrush, requiring somewhat moister conditions and sandier soils. Rabbit-brush may also be mistaken for sagebrush, both being medium-sized shrubs with gray, woolly hairs, or pubescence. However, rabbit-brush lacks the strong sage odor and has narrow (linear), non-lobed leaves. Most identifiable are rabbit-brush's more colorful, yellow disk flowers in showy clusters of small heads. The plants become very conspicuous when they bloom in late summer. The name *"chrysothamnus"* is of Greek derivation, meaning golden shrub. The fruits are capped with many bristles that aid in seed dissemination.

Two large and variable species of rabbit-brush thrive more or less throughout the sagebrush steppe. The most common of these is **gray rabbit-brush** (*Chrysothamnus nauseosus*), the specific epithet, *nauseosus*, meaning "heavy scented." White or gray woolly hairs densely cover the stems and leaves. This species often forms expansive populations, especially in the high plains and on sandy soils.

A second, common species of rabbit-brush is **green rabbit-brush** (*Chrysothamnus viscidiflorus*) which lacks woolly pubescence and, thus, appears greener. It has somewhat sticky, or viscid, stems and flowers. The two species of rabbit-brush often occur together. The plants provide poor quality browse for jackrabbits in spite of the common name; perhaps the rabbits hide in it rather than eat it. Deer, antelope, and other range animals feed sparingly on the leaves, flowers, and young twigs.

Oregon sunshine   *Eriophyllum lanatum*

Oregon sunshine is a very attractive plant with bright golden-yellow flowers and whitish-woolly leaves. The plants usually grow low and cushion-like but may be as much as two feet tall. They have several stems, each with one or a few showy heads consisting of rather conspicuous, green, outer involucral bracts, six to fourteen rays, and several disk flowers. The Latin name well describes this species: in Greek *erio* means wool and *phyllum* means leaf; *lanatum* also refers to wool. The woolly leaves are long and slender and usually divided into narrow segments. Oregon sunshine can easily be distinguished from daisies and goldenweeds by its rays which are darker yellow toward their base.

Oregon sunshine thrives in a variety of habitats, most frequently in dry sandy plains or on fine talus slopes. Widespread in the steppeland, it extends upward onto dry rocky sites in forest openings and along ridges. It flowers in late spring or early summer.

Rabbit-brush community

Gray rabbit-brush   *Chrysothamnus nauseosus*

Oregon sunshine   *Eriophyllum lanatum*

Balsamroot   *Balsamorhiza* species

The sunflower-like balsamroots (in Greek, *balsama* means balsam and *rhiza*, means root) are among the most colorful associates of sagebrush in the high plains. In the spring their bright sunny faces provide a brilliant splash of yellow over broad expanses of the sagebrush steppe. They are distinctive plants with rather large heart-shaped or divided basal leaves and several leafless (or nearly so) flowering stems. Each stem supports a single large head two to four inches across bearing showy, outer rays and numerous inner disk flowers. The roots are thick and carrot-like, though somewhat woody, and although they have a rather bitter flavor, they were eaten by Plains Indians.

The balsamroots exemplify the monkey wrench that plant hybridization introduces to the species concept. For over a hundred years a species has been defined as a group of closely related, interbreeding organisms that as a group are morphologically distinct and reproductively isolated from other such groups. By definition, then, species cannot interbreed, or hybridize.

However, many "species" do not unambiguously fit our definition of a species. Evolutionary divergence is more or less gradual and variation tends to be continuous among related plants. Thus, the assignment of species, the determination of where to "draw the line" becomes rather arbitrary, especially when reproductive isolation has not been achieved or is incomplete. A further complication is that many species are *products* of hybridization between other (parental) species, followed by chromosome doubling. An estimated fifty percent of plant species have developed in this way!

Frequently, "species" that are morphologically distinct (good "morphological species") freely hybridize and produce fertile offspring. Are these plant groups then not good species? Balsamroots exemplify this taxonomic dilemma. There are a number of more or less morphologically distinct but genetically similar balsamroots that regularly hybridize when their ranges overlap. In most cases, the hybrids are of little consequence because they are ecologically maladapted. Still the hybrids complicate our concepts of species. Two morphologically distinct species that routinely hybridize are **arrow-leaf balsamroot (*Balsamorhiza sagittata*)**, which grows in deep soil, and **Hooker's balsamroot (*Balsamorhiza hookeri*)**, which prefers lithosol. The hybrids appear along the border, or ecotone, of the very different habitats and cannot advance into either.

Arrow-leaf balsamroot   *Balsamorhiza sagittata*

Hybrid of arrow-leaf and Hooker's balsamroot
Hooker's balsamroot   *Balsamorhiza hookeri*

The most common and widespread of the balsamroots is **arrow-leaf balsamroot** (*Balsamorhiza sagittata*). Its arrowhead-shaped leaves are as much as twelve inches long, half as wide, and covered with fine woolly hair that gives them a grayish appearance. As is true in all balsamroots, the primary leaves appear at the base, although there may be one or two smaller, lance-shaped leaves below the head on the otherwise leafless flowering stalk. The plant may occasionally produce more than one head per stalk. Arrow-leaf balsamroot grows mostly in deep, sandy soil, and its range extends from the steppe upward into open, ponderosa pine forests and sagebrush-dominated mountain ridges. It often forms dense, rather spectacular populations.

Another common, and probably more drought tolerant, balsamroot of Washington and Oregon, especially the Columbia Basin, is **Carey's balsamroot** (*Balsamorhiza careyana*).This species can be distinguished from arrow-leaf balsamroot by its more heart-shaped, non-woolly, "varnished" leaves.

Other common steppe balsamroots have deeply lobed or divided (pinnate), more elongate leaves. Perhaps the most common among these is **Hooker's balsamroot** (*Balsamorhiza hookeri*). This low plant produces several finely divided, basal leaves and one to several leafless stems, each bearing a single attractive head two to three inches across. Hooker's balsamroot regularly inhabits dry rocky (lithosol) habitats more or less throughout the steppeland.

A similar though slightly larger species is **hoary balsamroot** (*Balsamorhiza incana*), a densely woolly (hoary) plant that requires more moisture than other species. It ranges from northeastern Oregon across Wyoming.

Large-leaf balsamroot (*Balsamorhiza macrophylla*) is a robust species with deeply divided compound leaves up to two feet long. The leaf segments, or leaflets, are long and narrow; the heads also large, are three to four inches across. This species commonly grows on the high, relatively moist steppelands and mountain ridges of Idaho, Utah, and Wyoming. Frequently it overlaps in distribution with arrow-leaf balsamroot, and the two occasionally hybridize.

The most unusual and rare of the balsamroots is **rosy balsamroot** (*Balsamroot rosea*). In this species, the rays turn from yellow to rose with age. In habit it resembles Hooker's balsamroot but the leaves are less finely divided. Rosy balsamroot's distribution is restricted to the lithosols of southeastern Washington. Its range overlaps with that of Carey's balsamroot, with which it freely hybridizes.

Arrow-leaf balsamroot panorama *Balsamorhiza sagittata*

Carey's balsamroot *Balsamorhiza careyana*

Rosy balsamroot *Balsamroot rosea*

Wyethia   *Wyethia* **species**

This small genus of plants has very large heads with yellow or white rays. The plants are herbaceous with leafy stems and large taproots. The genus honors Nathaniel Wyeth, a western North American explorer from the early nineteenth century.

The most common and widespread species is **northern wyethia** or **mule's ears** (*Wyethia amplexicaulis*). Few species can match the color and panoramic beauty of mule's ears. The large showy heads of bright yellow ray and disk flowers resemble those of balsamroots in color and size, creating some confusion between the two species. The plants also overlap in distribution. However, mule's ears proves easily distinguishable by a combination of the following characteristics: (1) the leaves are long, elliptical and pointed, resembling the ears of a mule, and grow on the stem as well as at the base of the plant; 2) mule's ears produces two or more heads per stem, the central one larger than the others; 3) the plant is totally hairless and appears brightly varnished, especially the green, resinous involucral bracts at the base of the heads. The stem leaves also clasp the stem as the specific epithet suggests (*amplex* means clasping, *caulis* means stem).

Mule's ears grows in sandy loam or gravel, sometimes with sagebrush but often in more moist, meadow-like areas. It is particularly abundant in the high plains, especially in Nevada, where its displays prove most spectacular. Due to its very wide range, however, mule's ears can be found in suitable habitats throughout the steppeland.

A very dissimilar, equally attractive species is **white-rayed wyethia** (*Wyethia helianthoides*). It differs from mule's ears by being somewhat hairy and producing usually solitary heads with one- to two-inch white rays. This species also grows in moist, meadow-like areas, often in dense populations in the high plains of the Rocky Mountains.

Blanket-flower   *Gaillardia aristata*

The blanket-flower's distinctive heads, each bearing approximately twelve attractive wedge-shaped rays, identify this species. The yellow ray flowers, about one inch long, have a purplish base and three prominent lobes. The center of the head, comprised of disk flowers, is brownish-purple. These rather tall plants grow up to three feet, producing few to several stems. Each stem bears a single head and a number of elongate leaves, the upper ones usually toothed or lobed.

Blanket-flower occupies a wide range and frequently grows in dense populations as a roadside weed. In the sagebrush steppe it inhabits the moister plains and dry meadows. Gardeners frequently cultivate blanket-flower (black-eyed susan) as an ornamental. It grows very well under non-competitive conditions.

Northern wyethia or mule's ears   *Wyethia amplexicaulis*

White-rayed wyethia   *Wyethia helianthoides*

Blanket-flower   *Gaillardia aristata*

Gold star   *Crocidium multicaule*

A small, slender annual, the gold star seldom grows more than six inches tall. Each of the one or more erect stems bears a single head. The leaves are mostly basal (being reduced upward on the stem), often toothed, and have a tuft of hair where leaf meets stem. The generic name comes from the Greek *crocid* which means "loosely woven cloth or wool" and relates to the woolly hair in the leaf-stem juncture. The bright golden-yellow rays, 1/4 to 1/2 inch long, usually number eight. The central disk flowers are also yellow. As the seeds, or achenes, mature, the receptacle elongates and becomes cone shaped.

Although these small plants are not particularly showy individually, their often very dense populations provide a spectacular display of bright color in early spring when very few steppe species are flowering. The distribution of gold star follows the sagebrush plains and open forests on the east side of the Cascade Range in Oregon and Washington.

Nipple-seed   *Thelysperma subnudum*

Nipple-seed is one of the most beautiful of the many sunflower-like plants of the sagebrush steppe. It has bright golden-yellow rays surrounded by attractive green bracts that are fused at the base to form a cup-shaped structure with triangular lobes. The unusual white, papery edges of the lobes contrast with the green bracts and the yellow flowers. The plant's one or more, four- to twelve-inch stems each bear a single showy head. The basal leaves are divided into long and narrow (linear) segments. The smaller stem leaves are mostly undivided and grow opposite each other on the stem.

Thelysperma is a Greek word meaning nipple-seed, describing the many minute, nipple-like projections coating the wall of the seed. *Subnudum* refers to the almost nude (leafless) stem. The species inhabits very dry rocky habitats in the hills and plains of the southern Rockies, from Wyoming through Utah and Colorado to Arizona and New Mexico. Nipple-seed grows most commonly in open juniper woodlands where it flowers in early summer.

Orange sneezeweed   *Helenium hoopesii*

The orange sneezeweed, with its unusually colored orange heads and its tall (up to three feet) stems, attracts special attention in its surroundings. The stems, typically clustered and branched, have a number of elongate, strongly veined leaves. The showy heads may be as much as three inches across with orange or yellowish rays and disk flowers.

Although ranging from southeastern Oregon through Nevada, Utah, Colorado, and Wyoming, this species is seldom common but usually represented by scattered individuals. Orange sneezeweed grows most prominently on mountain ridges and in open forests but extends downward onto high, moist sagebrush plains.

Helenium is an ancient Greek name given to some plant, perhaps a relative to orange sneezeweed, presumably in honor of Helen of Troy. The common name relates to its hay-fever-producing capability. It is poisonous to livestock.

Gold star and bitterbrush community

Nipple-seed *Thelysperma subnudum*
Orange sneezeweed *Helenium hoopesii*

Blepharipappus   *Blepharipappus scaber*

Although this species has no widely accepted common name, it is widespread and rather attractive. The representative plants are small, usually branched annuals that vary in height from a few to several inches, depending on growth conditions. The very narrow leaves alternate on the stem. Small heads support three to eight broad, white, three-lobed, petal-like rays. The disk flowers, about ten per head, are also white with contrasting purple anthers. The plants produce one to several flower heads, again depending on growth conditions. The species name describes the feathery segments, or pappus, of the seed head (*blepharis* means eyelash in Greek) and the stiff (scabrous) hair covering the plant. Blepharipappus grows most frequently in loose, somewhat sandy soils, widely distributed through the western part of the steppeland, extending east to central Idaho and Nevada.

A closely related, similarly distributed annual is **Tidytips** (*Layia glandulosa*). This plant differs from blepharipappus in having somewhat broader and often toothed leaves and yellow rather than white disc flowers. Tidytips also tends to be covered with resinous or sticky, or glandular, hair, as the specific epithet suggests. The common name derives from the "tidiness" of the three-lobed rays.

Rosy everlasting   *Antennaria rosea*

A number of species of everlasting (*Antennaria*) dot the sagebrush steppe, but none are as attractive as the widespread and variable rosy everlasting. This low, mat-forming plant spreads by runners. The small but numerous leaves mostly crowd on very short shoots. Erect flowering stems, up to twelve inches tall, have several narrow leaves and support a dense cluster of small heads that resemble the toes of a kitten, hence the popular name "pussytoes." Each head consists of many very small, unisexual flowers surrounded by attractive, thin and papery, white to rose red bracts. The name "everlasting" characterizes the texture and coloration of these bracts, a quality that makes pussytoes a nice addition to floral arrangements. Dense wool on the stem and leaves gives the entire plant a grayish tint.

Rosy everlasting grows commonly in the high sagebrush plains of the Rocky Mountains and eastern Cascades from Canada to California and New Mexico. Its range extends upward to open pine and Douglas fir forests and often to dry rocky, alpine ridges. The bracts tend to be redder at higher elevations. Throughout its range, rosy everlasting flowers in early summer, but the gray foliage remains attractive through the fall.

Blepharipappus
Blepharippapus scaber

Tidytips
Layia glandulosa

Rosy everlasting   Antennaria rosea

Groundsel
Senecio species

The very large *Senecio* genus includes many species in North America, mostly growing in mountain meadows or on montane talus slopes. Although somewhat daisy-like, groundsels appear flat-topped due to the several small, yellow heads borne near the tips of equal-height branches. In most cases the heads contain both ray and disk flowers. Unlike daisies, groundsels have only one set of equal-sized involucral bracts surrounding the heads. Species of *Senecio* contain poisonous alkaloids but are sufficiently unpalatable that livestock seldom eat them.

One of the most widely distributed groundsels of the sagebrush steppe is **gray groundsel** (*Senecio canus*). This attractive plant produces several six- to eighteen-inch-long stems bearing a few to several bright yellow heads. The many basal leaves have long leaf stalks and oblong blades that broaden toward the tip. Leaf edges lack teeth, an unusual trait among the groundsels. The stem leaves are reduced, the upper ones becoming bract-like. Grayish wool covers at least the undersides of the leaves. The stems are also moderately woolly. Gray groundsel commonly grows in the high plains and extends well up into the mountains along open ridges.

The most variable groundsel is **western groundsel** (*Senecio integerrimus*), much taller and coarser than gray groundsel. Derived from a shallow, fibrous root system, this species produces one or a few stems, each with several flower heads. The leaves, primarily basal, vary from typically egg-shaped to pinnately divided. Western groundsel occupies a variety of habitats, from sagebrush plains to alpine ridges. It grows more or less throughout the steppe, being most common in relatively moist sites.

Horse-brush
Tetradymia species

Three similar and closely related species of *Tetradymia* are widely distributed in the dry lands of western North America, especially in the Great Basin. All are small to medium-sized shrubs that closely resemble rabbit-brush (*Chrysothamnus*) but are coarser shrubs usually growing in drier sites. In some areas, especially in southern Idaho, Wyoming, Nevada, and Utah, horse-brush becomes a major dominant that forms extensive, dense populations that replace or intermingle with sagebrush.

The stems of horse-brush are brittle and usually whitish with short, dense, woolly hairs. The numerous small, narrow leaves are sometimes modified into vicious spines, as in **spiny horse-brush** (*Tetradymia spinosa*). The heads lack rays, and the disk flowers are small but bright yellow.

Although essentially non-palatable, and thus rarely eaten, horse-brush is highly poisonous, causing liver injury and extreme sensitivity to light when ingested. In the latter case, a pigment from horse-brush gets into the peripheral circulatory system and causes acute "sunburn" and extensive swelling around the head and neck in light-colored animals, especially white sheep. In extreme cases death may result from a combination of liver injury and sun damage.

Gray groundsel
Senecio canus

Western groundsel
Senecio integerrimus

Spiny horse-brush *Tetradymia spinosa*

Foothills arnica　　　　　　　　　*Arnica sororia*

The arnicas stand apart from most related members of the sunflower family in that they have opposite, or paired, rather than alternate leaves. Also, most of the several species of western arnicas grow in subalpine and alpine habitats, *A. sororia* being somewhat exceptional with its foothills and high plains distribution.

Foothills arnica has typical, bright yellow, sunflower-like heads with outer rays and inner disk flowers. The solitary stems reach one to two feet tall, with one head (rarely more) and two or three pairs of small opposite leaves. The basal leaves, much larger and more numerous than the stem leaves, have conspicuous parallel veins.

Although it often invades meadows, foothills arnica most frequently grows in rather dry, gravelly soils of sagebrush communities, in regions of cold winters and moist springs. It is widely distributed in southern and eastern Idaho, the high plains of Wyoming, and the northern part of the Great Basin.

Yarrow　　　　　　　　　*Achillea millefolium*

Few species have adapted as successfully to such a wide variety of habitats as has yarrow. Its ecological success is attributable to the evolution of a number of "environmental specialists," or ecotypic races. Representative races occupy almost all habitats from the desert to the alpine tundra, except forests and wet areas. Yarrow also has a wide geographical distribution, growing throughout the sagebrush steppe.

The individual plants usually grow somewhat more than one foot tall, often producing several stems. The leaves are very finely divided and fern-like; the lower leaves have leaf stalks (petioles) and are longer than the upper, non-petiolate ones. The small heads crowd into a flat-topped to rounded, umbrella-like cluster. Each head has three to five white rays.

One of the most outstanding characteristics of yarrow is its odor, particularly that of the crushed leaves. The dried leaves have a "minty" flavor and are occasionally used in tea. Yarrow also has a long history of medicinal use. It was named after Achilles who presumably used extracts from the plant to treat the wounds of his soldiers in the battle of Troy.

Utah thistle　　　　　　　　　*Cirsium utahense*

This is one of the few non-weedy, native species of thistle in western North America. It has rather large white to pale pink heads and very spiny leaves and involucral bracts. White, woolly hair covers the stems and leaves. Utah thistle grows througout the Great Basin, from eastern Washington and Oregon through Utah, from rather dry plains upward onto non-forested mountain slopes.

Foothills arnica   *Arnica sororia*   Yarrow   *Achillea millefolium*

Utah thistle   *Cirsium utahense*

Chaenactis

Chaenactis douglasii

Chaenactis is a variable and common biennial or short-lived perennial with stiffly erect stems and long, narrow taproots. The leaves, finely divided and fern-like, grow largest and most numerous near the base of the stem. Usually, the plants are somewhat woolly or glandular-sticky or both. Each plant bears a few to several heads singly at the ends of slender branches. The small but attractive tubular disk flowers are white to pinkish, densely congested in the heads that lack ray flowers.

Chaenactis inhabits dry, sandy or gravelly sites where it becomes inconspicuous because of its sand-colored heads and pale, woolly stems and leaves. It grows more or less throughout the sagebrush steppe, extending upward onto open rocky ridges in the mountains.

False dandelion

Agoseris glauca

False dandelion takes on a number of variant forms and inhabits non-forested areas from the sagebrush plains to alpine meadows. Also geographically widespread, it grows throughout western North America. The common name describes this plant's dandelion-like appearance. It has slender (more so than dandelion), erect, leafless stems, each with a single head of bright yellow rays, which sometimes turn pinkish with age. The seeds, or achenes, become parachute-like when mature and scatter widely on the wind. The leaves are all basal and narrowly lance-shaped, occasionally divided like those of dandelions. When torn the tissue exudes a rather bitter milky juice. The juice solidifies into a rubber-like material that can be chewed as gum, a use some Plains Indians apparently discovered. Unlike the dandelion, *Agoseris* is not an aggressive weed, and we therefore find it more attractive.

Microseris

Microseris troximoides

This is an occasional but widespread plant that also resembles the common dandelion in many respects. Its leafless stem supports a single dandelion-like head of bright yellow ray flowers; disk flowers are absent. Each of the seeds, or achenes, has a "parachute" that aids in wind dissemination. The leaves, narrow and strap-like with wavy edges, are sparsely to densely covered with woolly pubescence. The roots are mostly unbranched.

Although microseris is a rather attractive plant, its flowering heads close early in the day, especially during hot weather, and the plant then becomes inconspicuous and non-showy. It most frequently grows in dry, somewhat sandy soil, more or less throughout the sagebrush steppe. It flowers early in the spring.

Chaenactis *Chaenactis douglasii*   **False dandelion** *Agoseris glauca*

Microseris *Microseris troximoides*

Hawksbeard   *Crepis* species

Because species of *Crepis* closely resemble the ubiquitous dandelion, their beauty is often not appreciated. Most steppe hawksbeards are rather tall plants, up to two feet, with branched stems and showy, dandelion-like heads of yellow ray flowers. The seeds, or achenes, also resemble those of dandelion with their "parachutes" that aid in wind dissemination. The leaves, borne mainly at the base of the stem, are usually deeply divided into narrow, pointed segments.

Several species of *Crepis* occupy the sagebrush steppe, varying considerably in head size and general habit. The two species pictured here represent the extremes: **long-leaf hawksbeard** (***Crepis acuminatus***), tall with small, 3/4-inch heads and **low hawksbeard** (***Crepis modocensis***), low with large, two-inch heads. Long-leaf hawksbeard grows throughout the steppe in sandy to coarse gravelly soil. Low hawksbeard has a more limited distribution, Oregon to Montana, and prefers rocky soils. Its very large heads undoubtedly relate to the fact that it is a polyploid species. Doubling of chromosome numbers typically leads to "gigas" characteristics.

Two other common steppe species are *Crepis atrabarba*, a widespread species similar to long-leaf hawksbeard but with somewhat larger heads, and *Crepis barbigera*, common in Washington, Oregon, and eastern Idaho. The latter species probably evolved through hybridization between *Crepis atrabarba* and *Crepis modocensis*, being intermediate between these two species, especially in head size. The individual plants are largely sterile, suggesting hybrid origin. All of the hawksbeards flower in early summer.

Prairie pink   *Lygodesmia grandiflora*

Most plains species of the sunflower family have either disk flowers or yellow rays or both. Prairie pink is therefore distinctive in lacking disk flowers and having pink to lavender-blue rays. The plants grow four to twelve inches tall with thin flexuous stems (in Greek *lygos* means pliant or limber twig and *desmia* means bundle and relates to the frequently clustered stems). The leaves, very narrow or linear, roll inward at the edges, and are reduced in size upward on the stems. Each stem produces one or few heads with six to fifteen showy, one to two inch rays.

Prairie pink grows on gravelly hills and in sandy plains east of the Continental Divide in Wyoming, Colorado, and Utah. It flowers in early summer, sometimes creating large and beautiful displays.

Long-leaf hawksbeard
Crepis acuminatus

Low hawksbeard
Crepis modocensis

Prairie pink *Lygodesmia grandiflora*

Weeds of the Sunflower Family

The sunflower family not only includes the largest number of native plants in the sagebrush steppe, but is also one of three large families of weeds—the others being the mustard and grass families. Although this book focuses on native species and natural communities, the impact of introduced weeds cannot be ignored. In some areas of the steppe, the native vegetation has largely been replaced by invasive weeds, especially where overgrazing or other abusive activities have disrupted the habitat.

By far, the worst weeds of the sagebrush steppe are the **knapweeds** of the genus *Centaurea*, in the sunflower family. Species of knapweeds combine a broad ecological tolerance with an unusual competitive ability. Plants sharing these "qualities" inevitably become noxious weeds. Many thousands of acres of rangeland have been overrun by knapweeds, greatly reducing the commercial and aesthetic value of the land.

The three most widespread of the knapweeds are **spotted knapweed** (*Centaurea maculosa*), **yellow starthistle** (*Centaurea solstitialis*), and **diffuse knapweed** (*Centaurea diffusa*), probably in that order. Spotted knapweed, a perennial, has spread over much of the northern steppeland, especially in Montana. Probably more cold tolerant than the other species, it reaches higher into the mountains. Yellow starthistle is an annual that competes very successfully for limited moisture. It has become a major problem in much of Oregon and southern Idaho. Diffuse knapweed, a biennial or short-lived perennial with white or pale lavender flowers, is most prevalent in central and eastern Washington. All of the knapweeds have attractive heads that resemble those of bachelor buttons, of the same genus. Knapweeds lack rays, but the peripheral disk flowers are often elongate, in this respect being ray-like. The species also provide an excellent source of nectar for bees and other insects in mid to late summer when other nectar sources are scarce. However, the virtues of these weeds are far outweighed by the ecological damage they have done and continue to do.

Many other weedy members of the sunflower family grow in the sagebrush steppe, some also highly invasive, including musk and Scotch thistles. For a detailed treatment of weeds of the steppe, and the Northwest as a whole, see *Northwest Weeds* by Ronald Taylor, published by Mountain Press Publishing Company of Missoula, Montana.

Spotted knapweed
Centaurea maculosa

Diffuse knapweed
Centaurea diffusa

Yellow starthistle *Centaurea solstitialis*

SYRINGA FAMILY

Hydrangeaceae

Syringa

Philadelphus lewisii

Syringa is an extensively branched, medium-sized shrub that frequents coarse talus slopes and rocky ledges, particularly along canyon walls and dry gullies. This extremely attractive shrub bears numerous, rather large, very fragrant white flowers. From a distance it resembles and is often mistaken for serviceberry (*Amelanchier*), which may occupy similar habitats. Syringa can easily be distinguished, however, by one or a combination of the following characteristics: the leaves and branches are opposite (paired at the nodes); the fruits form woody capsules rather than berries; the leaves are heavily veined and non-toothed; and most importantly, the flowers have only four rather than five petals. Like serviceberry, syringa provides preferred browse for deer.

Syringa ranges from British Columbia through Washington and Oregon and east to Montana. It is widely distributed in northern Idaho and is the State flower.

Philadelphus is of Greek derivation (*philos* means love, *delphos* means brother) and the genus was named in honor of Ptolemy II (Philadelphus), who ruled Egypt from 263 to 247 BC. *Philadelphus lewisii*, first collected by Lewis and Clark along the Bitterroot River in Montana, was named in honor of Meriwether Lewis. The common name, syringa, dates back to a time during the middle ages when this genus was combined with lilac in the genus *Syringa*.

Syringa   *Philadelphus lewisii*

VIOLET FAMILY

Violaceae

This family is characterized by its bilaterally symmetrical, pansy-like flowers. The flowers exhibit various styles of nectar guides and recognition color patterns.

Sagebrush violet

Viola trinervata

Violets and pansies typically inhabit cool, moist habitats of forests and meadows. However, sagebrush violet presents an exception in that it grows only in poorly developed soils amid rock formations. Here, the fleshy roots penetrate small crevices to moderate depths and absorb the spring moisture that collects. Flowers appear very early in the spring, and by summer the dormant plants have dried up and appear dead.

The very showy flowers of sagebrush violet, although somewhat smaller, closely resemble those of cultivated pansies. The two upper petals are reddish-violet; the three lower ones are lilac with purple lines and a yellowish base. The leaves are rather distinctive: somewhat fleshy and leathery and divided into a number of strongly veined leaflets or leaf segments. This species grows rather commonly in lithosol communities of central Washington and northern Oregon.

Yellow prairie violet

Viola nuttallii

This is probably the most variable violet of western North America. It varies in flower color, leaf shape, size, and habitat preference. Typically, it bears bright yellow petals with dark purple lines (nectar guides) leading to the mouth of the flower. A sac at the back of the flower conceals the nectar. The conspicuously veined leaves are one to four inches long, elliptical, and often slightly toothed. The plants range from the upper steppes into open forests and onto mountain ridges. In some varietal form yellow prairie violet exists more or less throughout the sagebrush steppe, except in the drier habitats.

Blue violet

Viola adunca

Blue violet is a small, low-growing plant with erect flowering stems up to three inches tall. The leaves are ovate to heart-shaped, usually toothed, and one half to one inch long and wide. The flowers, only about one half inch long, sport a conspicuous, narrow, nectar-containing spur that extends from the back of the flower. The typically blue-purple petals have darker stripes (nectar guides) leading to the center of the flower. Often the base of the petals, the "throat" of the flower, is lighter in color, sometimes white.

Blue violet grows throughout western North America, where a number of varieties are recognized. The plants range from the upper sagebrush prairies to moist meadows, extending upward through forests onto high mountain ridges. Blue violet blooms in late spring.

Sagebrush violet *Viola trinervata*

Yellow prairie violet *Viola nuttallii*
Blue violet *Viola adunca*

WATERLEAF FAMILY   Hydrophyllaceae

Dwarf waterleaf   *Hydrophyllum capitatum*

Dwarf waterleaf is an unusual but very attractive plant. It tends to be somewhat inconspicuous, however, because it usually grows amid thickets or beneath associated shrubs, such as sagebrush, and because the rather dark flowers blend in with the dull, shady background. The blue-purple to lavender flowers form a densely congested ball-shaped cluster near the base of the plant. The stamens extend well beyond the sepals and petals giving the inflorescence the appearance of a round brush. The leaves are pinnately compound with variously lobed leaflets. The stems and leaf stalks, or petioles, are somewhat soft and fleshy but there seems to be little justification for the name, *Hydrophyllum* (in Greek *hydro* means water and *phyllum* means leaf) unless it relates to the fact that the leaves tend to collect water that channels down the grooved petioles to the roots.

Dwarf waterleaf extends over a broad altitudinal range, from the high plains to subalpine meadows. It most often grows along the border between lower forest or woodland habitats and the sagebrush steppeland. However, it inhabits sites of sufficient spring moisture throughout the limits of the sagebrush steppe and flowers very early in the spring.

White-leafed phacelia   *Phacelia hastata*

White-leafed phacelia is the most variable and one of the least attractive of several species in the genus *Phacelia*. Its name comes from the silky-white hairiness of the leaves. The variation of the plants is expressed in terms of size, from a few inches to three feet, and flower color, from typically whitish to shades of blue in montane forms. The leaves are narrowly elliptical and many have a pair of lobes at the base of the blade. The upper leaves are smaller. The flowers crowd into a number of coiled clusters, called cymes, that appear bristly as a result of the extended stamens. The petals are fused into a "funnel" with five lobes.

White-leafed phacelia grows in the high plains and on mountain ridges throughout western North America. It prefers sandy or gravelly sites and flowers in early summer.

Narrow-leafed phacelia   *Phacelia linearis*

In moist years narrow-leafed phacelia becomes a common and beautiful plant. The often-branched stems reach up to eighteen inches tall and bear several pale lavender to dark blue showy flowers. In dry years, or in especially dry habitats, the plants remain small and unbranched with only one or a few pale lavender flowers. In either case, the leaves are narrow, elongate, and sometimes have two basal lobes; the petals are fused at the base, resembling a bowl, and have five projecting stamens.

Narrow-leafed phacelia, an annual plant, is widespread in the dry plains and foothills of western North America. It grows most frequently in sandy soils where it often forms rather dense populations. It flowers in the springtime.

Dwarf waterleaf *Hydrophyllum capitatum*

White-leafed phacelia
Phacelia hastata

Narrow-leafed phacelia
Phacelia linearis

171

Golden gilia   *Phacelia adenophora*

Golden gilia is a beautiful annual with many bright, golden-yellow or lavender-tinged flowers usually grouped near the ends of low spreading branches. The attractive pinnately divided leaves are concentrated near the base of the near-prostrate, branched stem. The petals, about 1/4 inch long, are fused at the base forming a "saucer" with five lobes. The five stamens and the base of the "saucer" are hairy.

Golden gilia inhabits the sagebrush zone of northeastern California and adjacent Oregon and Nevada. It grows in slightly alkaline areas where it frequently forms very dense and showy populations. It flowers in late May and early June.

Hesperochiron   *Hesperochiron pumilus*

Although this species has apparently never been given a common name, it well might be called "false strawberry" since it superficially resembles the wild strawberry. It is a low, spreading plant with white strawberry-like flowers. It has only five (rather than numerous) stamens, however, and the petals are fused at their base into a short, hairy-throated tube. The leaves—being non-lobed, fleshy, and elliptical—are also clearly distinct from those of strawberries.

This and other species of Hesperochiron inhabit swales or other moist sites more or less throughout the sagebrush steppe. Although fairly common, they are infrequently observed because they bloom only briefly in early spring and are often hidden beneath larger plants, such as sagebrush.

Golden gilia *Phacelia adenophora*

Hesperochiron *Hesperochiron pumilus*

WILLOW FAMILY   Salicaceae

This is a family of woody plants with simple, alternate leaves and dense spikes (catkins) of unisexual flowers. The ovary develops into a capsule that splits open at maturity, releasing hundreds of minute seeds with cottony appendages that catch the wind, allowing wide seed dispersal. Several species of **willow** (*Salix*) grow in and around meadow areas in the steppe. These are rather large shrubs.

Quaking aspen   *Populus tremuloides*

Quaking aspen hardly constitutes an element of the sagebrush steppe, yet it frequently inhabits the high plains and foothills along ravines or well-drained depressions where seepage often occurs early in the spring and the water table remains near the surface through the dry summer months. In these areas water comes primarily as melt from large snow drifts along the crests of the hills above. However, in spite of a greater availability of water here than in the surrounding sagebrush communities, these sites rarely become marshy or meadow-like. The deep and fertile sandy-loam soil of the aspen groves results from years of erosion of the upland slopes. The most frequent associates of aspen are large shrubs: chokecherry, serviceberry, and hawthorn, all of which produce edible fruit. The aspen grove surrounded by a "sea" of sagebrush presents an impressive sight. The trees are rather tall and straight with conspicuously white bark and dark green, trembling or quaking leaves. In the fall, the leaves of aspen and associated shrubs provide a splash of golden color that contrasts sharply with the gray-green hue of the surrounding sagebrush. The aspen grove offers a haven for birds and wildlife, providing food, sometimes water, and shelter from insects, predators, humans, and adverse climate.

Aspen grove with sagebrush and mule's ears

Pussywillows
Salix phylicifolia

Quaking aspen and mule's ears in low, moist area (late spring)

APPENDIX I

Key for the Identification of Representative Families

Although attempting to use an identification key may be a frustrating experience for the botanical novice, familiarity with the key and with plant structures in general should resolve most difficulties. Knowledge of plant structures can be supplemented by reference to the descriptive illustrations (page 189) and glossary (page 194). Familiarity with the key can be gained only through experience.

The key presented here is dichotomous or two-branched; that is, at every position in the key, the user has two mutually exclusive choices, "a" and "b" of the same number. In the identification of a plant, the user should start at the beginning of the key, and always progress forward (never backward), choosing only between the two descriptions ("a" and "b") of each numerical set (dichotomy) until the selected choice refers to a family and page where the species of that family are pictured and described in the text. A few helpful notes in the utilization of this key are: (1) the choice must be between the "a" and "b" of the same number; (2) the descriptions of "a" and "b" should be read carefully before making a choice; (3) after choosing between "a" and "b" proceed to the numerical dichotomy indicated until you have identified the family; (4) qualifying words such as "mostly," "often," "usually," etc. mean what they say and should not be ignored.

To make the use of the key easier, family descriptions are based primarily on representatives from the sagebrush steppe. If all species of a family were taken into consideration, the variation would be much greater and, accordingly, the families would be much more difficult to key out.

1a. Fragrant shrubs with twisted and gnarled stems; leaves wedge-shaped with three shallow or deep lobes; coloration gray-green from a dense covering of minute, woolly hair
Sagebrush (*Artemisia* species) page 18

1b. Plants with various characteristics but not in the same combination as above .... 2.

2a. Leafless, green shrubs with stiffly erect and jointed, broom-like branches; flowers not produced .... **Ephedra family (Ephedraceae) page 44**

177

2b. Plants having green leaves OR otherwise not as above .... 3.

3a. Plants spiny and leafless, thick and succulent, round and unbranched or branches flattened and jointed; flowers showy
Cactus family (cactaceae) page 38

3b. Plants not spiny OR otherwise not as above .... 4.

4a. Non-green (brownish) parasitic plants with low, fleshy, clustered stems and scalelike leaves
Broomrape family (Orobanchaceae) page 26

4b. Plant with green leaves although these sometimes very small and/or covered with whitish hair .... 5.

5a. Flowers densely congested into heads with greenish outer bracts, the heads sunflower-like or daisy-like (with outer ray flowers and inner disk flowers), dandelion-like (with only ray flowers), or chaenactis-like (with only disk flowers). See the illustrations
Sunflower family (Compositae) page 134

5b. Flowers not in heads but if apparently so, the heads not resembling a single flower as above .... 6.

6a. Trees or large shrubs (two feet tall or more); flowers not blue .... 7.

6b. Herbs or small shrubs (mostly less than 2 feet tall) flowers sometimes blue ....11.

7a. Medium-sized, spiny shrubs with clustered, unisexual, mostly inconspicuous flowers
Goosefoot family (Chenopodiaceae) (in part) page 64

7b. Plants rarely spiny; flowers usually conspicuous .... 8.

8a. Leaves and branches opposite; flowers showy with four white petals.
Syringa family (Hydrangeaceae) page 166

8b. Leaves and branches alternate; flowers not showy OR if so, petals 5 . 9.

9a. Trees or large shrubs with entire (non-toothed nor lobed) leaves (including quaking aspen, a tree with white bark)
Willow family (Salicaceae) page 174

9b. Shrubs with toothed or lobed leaves .... 10.

10a. Leaves lobed and maple-like in outline; sepals more showy than petals
Currant family (Grossulariaceae) page 42

10b. Leaves toothed or shallowly lobed but hardly maplelike; petals more showy than sepals.........**Rose family (Rosaceae)** (in part) **page 124**

11a. Grass-like herbs with hollow, joined stems and long, narrow leaves with parallel veins; flowers reduced and not obvious
Grass family (Gramineae) page 68

11b. Stems and leaves NOT BOTH as above; flowers usually obvious when present..12.

12a. Sepals and petals 3 each, mostly similar in size and color (the style branches flattened and petal-like in iris); leaves mostly basal, long and narrow (sometimes round) with parallel veins; plants not woody..13.

12b. Sepals and petals usually more than 3 each and seldom similar in size and color (if so, plants woody at the base); leaves various but usually not as above. ....14.

13a. Stamens 6; ovary superior; plants producing bulbs.
Lily family (Liliaceae) page 74

13b. Stamens 3; ovary inferior; plants not producing bulbs
Iris family (Iridaceae) page 72

14a. Petals 4; flowers regular (radially symmetrical), usually showy .....15.

14b. Petals more or less than 4 (sometimes none); flowers sometimes irregular (bilaterally symmetrical) and sometimes inconspicuous ....18.

15a. Stamens 8 (4 of the 8 sometimes shorter and poorly developed); flower parts usually borne on a long, narrow tube from the top of the ovary (ovary inferior) ..**Evening primrose family (Onagraceae) page 44**

15b. Stamens 4 or 6; flower parts borne on the receptacle, at the base of the ovary (ovary superior) ....16.

16a Stamens 4; petals small and papery; flowers borne in a dense spike.
Plantain family (Plantaginaceae) page 118

16b. Stamens 6; petals mostly showy and not papery; flowers borne in racemes ....17.

17a. Leaves palmately compound; stamens extended well beyond the petals
Caper family (Capparidaceae) page 40

17b. Leaves not palmately compound; stamens usually not extended beyond the petals ....**Mustard family (Cruciferae) page 88**

18a. Flowers inconspicuous; plants spiny OR white woolly
Goosefoot family (Chenopodiaceae) (in part) page 64

18b. Flowers usually conspicuous OR if not, plants neither spiny nor white woolly...19.

19a. Petals 6, white and showy; plants prickly
Poppy family (Papaveraceae) page 118

19b. Petals not 6 OR if so, NOT white; plants usually not prickly ....20.

20a. Petals and sepals 3 each (or petals absent); flowers usually borne in umbels or heads; plants usually woody at the base
Buckwheat family (Polygonaceae) page 28

20b. Petals and sepals more or less than 3 each; flowers not borne in umbels or heads OR if so, petals 5 and plants not woody. ....21.

21a. Upper leaves (or bracts) and sepals reddish or yellowish, more showy than the petals
Figwort family (Scrophulariaceae) (in part) page 48

21b. Upper leaves green, not otherwise conspicuously pigmented ....22.

22a. Flowers clearly irregular (bilaterally symmetrical) ....23.

22b. Flowers regular (radially symmetrical) or nearly so ....27.

23a. Stamens more than 10; sepals blue, showy and with a single spur
Buttercup family (Ranunculaceae) (in part) page 34

23b. Stamens 10 or fewer; sepals green or reddish ....24.

24a. Flowers sweetpea-like; leaves pinnately or palmately compound; stamens 10 ....**Pea family (Leguminosae) page 100**

24b. Flowers not pea-like; leaves rarely compound; stamens 5 or fewer ....25.

25a. Flowers pansy-like; plants prostrate often with divided leaves
Viola family (Violaceae) page 168

25b. Flowers not pansy-like; plants taller OR if not, leaves not
divided ....26.

26a. Bushy shrubs with a strong minty odor, or herbs with square stems and
opposite leaves; ovary developing into 4 nutlets
Mint family (Labiatae) page 86

26b. Herbs or odorless shrubs; ovary developing into a many-seeded capsule
Figwort family (Scrophulariaceae) (in part) page 48

27a. Stamens numerous, far more than 10 per flower ....28.

27b. Stamens 10 or fewer. ....32.

28a. Flowers orange to red-orange; stamens fused at the base forming a tube
Mallow family (Malvaceae) page 84

28b. Flowers sometimes reddish but not orange; stamens not fused .... 29.

29a. Flowers pink, petals more than 5.
Purslane family (Portulacaceae) (in part) page 122

29b. Flowers not pink OR if so, petals 5 ....30.

30a. Flowers blue to purplish OR if yellow (buttercups) then plants prostrate
Buttercup family (Ranunculaceae) (in part) page 34

30b. Flowers yellow to reddish; plants erect...31.

31a. White-stemmed plants with sandpaper-like leaves
Loasa family (Loasaceae) page 82

31b. Plants neither white-stemmed nor with sandpaper-like leaves
Rose family (Rosaceae) (in part) page 124

32a. Leaves all basal (borne at ground level); petals reddish and turned
backward, away from the face of the flower
Primrose family (Primulaceae) page 120

32b. Leaves and flowers various but not combined as above...................33.

33a. Petals fused into a tube with 5 lobes (more or less trumpet-shaped), all
separating from the flower as a unit; stamens borne on (and inside) the
petal tube ....34.

33b. Petals not fused (sometimes absent), separating from the flower individually; stamens borne on the receptacle or ovary ....37.

34a. Erect plants with opposite leaves and slightly irregular, blue flowers
Figwort family (Scrophulariaceae) (in part) **page 48**

34b. Flowers clearly regular and not blue OR if blue, leaves either alternate or plants more or less prostrate ....35.

35a. Stamens extending well beyond the petals, giving the flower clusters a bristly appearance .. **Waterleaf family (Hydrophylaceae) page 170**

35b. Stamens included within or barely visible beyond the petal tubes ....36.

36a Plants usually bristly hairy; flowers usually borne in a coiled cluster; style not branched; ovary developing into 4 nutlets
Borage family (Boraginaceae) page 22

36b. Plants not bristly hairy; flowers not borne in a coiled cluster; style 3-branched; ovary developing into a capsule
Phlox family (Polemoniaceae) page 110

37a. Tall (2-3 feet) slender herbs with colorful, sky-blue flowers
Flax family (Linaceae) page 62

37b. Shorter plants with reddish, purplish, yellow, or white flowers ......38.

38a. Flowers borne in umbels; leaves divided and carrot-like
Parsley family (Umbelliferae) page 94

38b. Flowers not borne in umbels OR if apparently so, leaves not carrot-like ....39.

39a. Low succulent plants with star-shaped, yellow flowers
Stonecrop family (Crassulaceae) page 132
39b. Plants not both succulent and yellow-flowered ....40.

40a. Plants more than one foot tall with leafy stems and showy pink (or white) flowers ....**Geranium family (Geraniaceae) page 62**

40b. Plants not having the same combination of characters as above .....41.

41a. Dense cushion plants (not more than a few inches tall); flowers white
Pink family (Caryophyllaceae) page 116

41b. Plants not as described above .... 42.

42a. Sepals 2; plants rather fleshy with pink to white flowers and a pair of opposite stem leaves
Purslane family (Portulacaceae) (in part) **page 122**

42b. Sepals 5; plants not as described above .... 43.

43a. Leaves divided or lobed, mostly basal
Saxifrage family (Saxifragaceae) page 130

43b. Leaves entire, neither divided nor lobed
Sandalwood family (Santalaceae) page 128

APPENDIX II

Sagebrush steppe species are listed by vegetative zone that they most frequently inhabit. Some species grow regularly in two or more zones and therefore have multiple inclusions. Also, the zones (habitats) intergrade making the placement of species in particular zones somewhat arbitrary.

Standard-Type Zone
Achillea millefolium
Agoseris glauca
Agropyron spicatum
Allium acuminatum
Allium douglasii
Amsinckia retrorsa
Antennaria rosea
Arabis divaricarpa
Arabis holboellii
Arenaria aculeata
Arenaria capillaris
Argemone platyceras
Arnica sororia
Artemisia tridentata
Aster adscendens
Aster chilensis
Aster xylorrhiza
Astragalus arrectus
Astragalus crassicarpus
Astragalus filipes
Atriplex spinosa

Balsamorhiza careana
Balsamorhiza incana
Balsamorhiza macrophylla
Balsamorhiza sagittata
Blepharipappus scaber
Bouteloua gracilis
Brodiaea douglasii

Brodiaea howellii
Brodiaea hyacinthina
Bromus tectorum

Calochortus lyallii
Calochortus macrocarpus
Calochortus nuttallii
Castilleja angustifolia
Castilleja applegatei
Castilleja chromosa
Castilleja exilis
Castilleja linariaefolia
Castilleja sessiliflora
Castilleja thompsonii
Centaurea diffusa
Centaurea maculosa
Centaurea solstitialis
Chaenactis douglasii
Chrysothamnus nauseosus
Chrysothamnus viscidiflorus
Cirsium utahense
Clarkia pulchella
Claytonia lanceolata
Clematis hirsutissima
Cleome lutea
Cleome platycarpa
Collomia grandiflora
Collomia linearis
Comandra umbellata
Corydalis aurea

Cowania stansburiana
Crepis acuminatus
Crepis atribarba
Crepis barbigera
Crepis modocensis
Crocidium multicaule
Cryptantha flava
Cryptantha glomerata

Delphinium bicolor
Delphinium nuttallianum
Delphinium occidentale
Dodecatheon pauciflorum

Ephedra viridis
Erigeron aphanactis
Erigeron compositus
Erigeron engelmannii
Erigeron filifolius
Erigeron poliospermus
Erigeron pumilus
Eriogonum compositum
Eriogonum heracleoides
Eriogonum ovalifolium
Eriogonum strictum
Eriogonum umbellatum
Eriophyllum lanatum
Erysimum asperum
Erysimum occidentale

Festuca idahoensis
Fritillaria atropurpurea
Fritillaria pudica

Gaillardia aristata
Geranium richardsonii
Geranium viscosissimum
Geum triflorum
Gilia aggregata
Gutierrezia sarothrae

Hackellia arida
Hedysarum boreale
Helenium hoopesii
Hesperochiron pumilus
Hydrophyllum capitatum

Koeleria cristata

Lathyrus pauciflorus
Layia glandulosa
Linum perenne
Lithophragma bulbifera
Lithophragma parviflora
Lithospermum ruderale
Lomatium dissectum
Lomatium gormanii
Lomatium grayi
Lomatium nudicaule
Lomatium triternatum
Lupinus ammophilus
Lupinus sericeus
Lupinus sulphureus
Lupinus wyethii
Lygodesmia grandiflora

Mertensia longiflora
Microseris troximoides

Oenothera tanecetifolia
Opuntia polyacantha
Orobanche uniflora
Orobanche fasciculata
Orthocarpus barbatus
Orthocarpus hispidus
Orthocarpus luteus
Orthocarpus tenuifolius
Oxytropis sericea
Oxytropis lagopus

Penstemon alpinus
Penstemon cobaea
Penstemon cyaneus
Penstemon humilus
Penstemon speciosus
Penstemon whippleanus
Perideridia gairdneri
Phacelia adenophora
Phacelia hastata
Phlox longifolia
Phlox multiflora
Phlox speciosa
Physaria vitulifera

Plantago patagonica
Poa sandbergii
Populus tremuloides
Potentilla gracilis
Purshia tridentata

Ranunculus glaberrimus

Salsola kali
Scutellaria antirrhinoides
Senecio canus
Senecio integerrimus
Sisymbrium altissimum
Sisyrinchium angustifolium
Sisyrinchium douglasii
Sisyrinchium inflatum
Sphaeralcea coccinea
Sphaeralcea munroana
Stanleya pinnata

Tetradymia spinosa
Thelypodium laciniatum
Thelysperma subnudum
Townsendia florifer
Townsendia parryi

Viola nuttallii
Viola adunca

Wyethia amplexicaulis

Zygadenus venenosus

Lithosol Zone
Allium robinsonii
Arenaria hookeri
Artemisia rigida
Aster scopulorum
Astragalus purshii

Balsamorhiza hookeri
Balsamorhiza rosea

Corydalis aurea

Erigeron asperugineus

Erigeron compositum
Erigeron engelmannii
Erigeron linearis
Erigeron poliospermus
Eriogonum caespitosum
Eriogonum sphaerocephalum
Eriogonum thymoides

Gutierrezia sarothrae

Haplopappus acaulis
Haplopappus armerioides
Haplopappus stenophyllus

Leptodactylon pungens
Lewisia rediviva
Lomatium macrocarpum
Lomatium gormanii
Lupinus aridus

Mimulus cusickii

Oenothera caespitosa
Opuntia polyacantha
Oxytropis lagopus

Pediocactus simpsonii
Penstemon deustus
Penstemon gairdneri
Penstemon lariciflorus
Penstemon wilcoxii
Phlox hoodii
Phoenicaulis cheiranthoides
Poa secunda

Ranunculus glaberrimus

Sedum lanceolatum
Sedum stenopetalum

Townsendia florifer
Townsendia parryi
Trifolium macrocephalum

Viola trinervata

Sand Dune Zone
Arenaria franklinii
Astragalus succumbens

Blepharipappus scaber

Calochortus macrocarpus
Chaenactis douglasii
Chrysothamnus nauseosus
Chrysothamnus viscidiflorus
Cleome lutea
Comandra umbellata
Cryptantha flava
Cryptantha leucophylla

Erigeron filifolius
Erigeron pumilus
Eriogonum niveum
Eriogonum ovalifolium
Erysimum asperum

Layia glandulosa
Lesquerella douglasii
Linum perenne
Lupinus species

Mimulus cusickii
Mimulus nanus

Oenothera deltoides
Oenothera pallida
Oenothera trichocalyx
Opuntia polyacantha
Orthocarpus barbatus
Orthocarpus luteus
Oryzopsis hymenoides

Penstemon acuminatus
Penstemon speciosus
Phacelia hastata
Phacelia linearis
Phlox speciosa
Physaria vitulifera
Plantago patagonica
Purshia tridentata

Rumex venosus

Salsola kali

Talus Zone
Amelanchier alnifolia
Arabis holboellii
Argemone platyceras
Artemisia tridentata
Balsamorhiza sagittata

Ephedra viridis
Eriogonum compositum
Eriogonum heracleoides
Eriogonum niveum
Eriogonum ovalifolium
Eriophyllum lanatum

Gilia aggregata

Haplopappus armerioides
Heuchera cylindrica

Leptodactylon pungens
Lesquerella douglasii
Lomatium dissectum
Lomatium grayi
Lupinus sulphureus

Mentzelia laeviculmis

Oenothera brachycarpa
Oenothera caespitosa

Penstemon alpinus
Penstemon deustus
Penstemon eatonii
Penstemon humilus
Penstemon pruinosus
Penstemon richardsonii
Philadelphus lewisii
Phlox multiflora
Physaria vitulifera
Purshia tridentata

Ribes aureum
Ribes cereum

Salvia dorrii
Stanleya pinnata

Thelypodium laciniatum
Thelysperma subnuda

Meadow Zone
Camassia quamash
Carex species

Dodecatheon conjugens
Dodecatheon pulchellum

Iris missouriensis

Juncus species

Mimulus guttatus

Orobanche uniflora

Potentilla gracilis

Sisyrinchium angustifolium
Sisyrinchium douglasii
Sisyrinchium inflatum
Thermopsis montana

Salix species

Wyethia amplexicaulis
Wyethia helianthoides

Saline Zone
Atriplex spinosa

Castilleja exilis

Distichlis stricta

Eurotia lanata

Salsola kali
Sarcobatus vermiculatus

Complete Flower

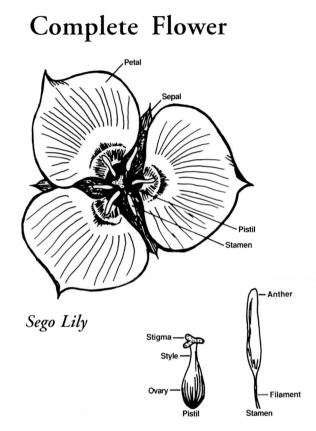

Sego Lily

Additional characteristics illustrated:
- Superior ovary
- Regular flower
- Radial symmetry
- Non-fused petals

Primary Inflorescence Types

Raceme

Tansy Mustard

Spike

Alumroot

Umbel

Desert Parsley

Head

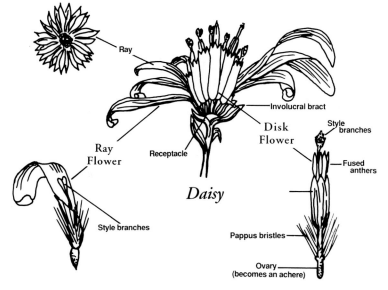

Ray

Ray Flower

Involucral bract

Receptacle

Disk Flower

Style branches

Fused anthers

Daisy

Style branches

Pappus bristles

Ovary (becomes an achere)

Flower Types

Radial Symmetry

Fused Petals

Non-Fused Petals

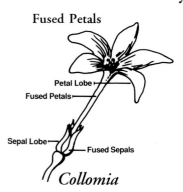

Petal Lobe

Fused Petals

Sepal Lobe

Fused Sepals

Collomia

Wild Geranium

Bilateral Symmetry

Fused Petals

Non-Fused Petals

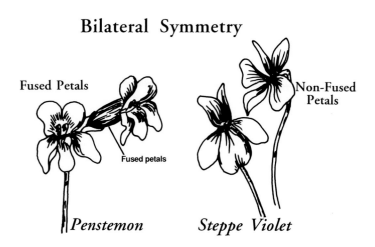

Fused petals

Penstemon

Steppe Violet

Leaf Type

Simple Leaves

Entire Leaf

Toothed Leaf

Palmately
Lobed Leaf

Shooting Star

Penstemon

Wild Geranium

Compound Leaves

Palmately
Compound Leaf

Leaflet

Petiole

Stipule

Lupine

Pinnately
Compound Leaf

Leaflet

Petiole

Stipule

Locoweed

Ovary Position

Inferior Ovary

Superior Ovary

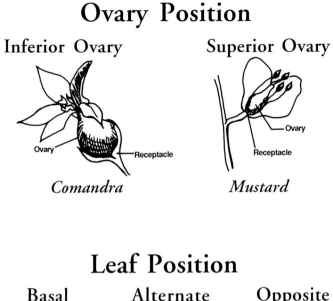

Comandra

Mustard

Leaf Position

Basal

Alternate

Opposite

*Desert
Buckwheat*

Fiddleneck

Penstemon

GLOSSARY

Achene — A small, hard, one-seeded fruit that functions as a single seed.

Alkaline — Basic as opposed to acidic; high pH.

Alkaloid — A toxic nitrogen-containing substance. Plants produce many different alkaloids that serve a defensive role, being poisonous to animals.

Alternate — As applied to leaves: not opposite, one leaf per node (see the illustrations).

Annual — A plant that lives only one year (from seed to seed in one year).

Anther — The part of the stamen (male sex organ) that produces the pollen.

Axil — The angle formed by a leaf with the stem (axillary).

Basal — As applied to leaves: at the base of the stem, at or near ground level.

Biennial — A plant that lives two years, the first year producing leaves and a thick taproot, the second year developing an erect stem with flowers.

Bilaterally symmetrical — Relating to a flower: irregular, with a left side and right side; mirror images can be produced only by dividing the flower in a vertical plane; one (or more) of the petals and/or sepals is (are) unlike others (see the illustrations).

Blade — The flat part of a leaf or petal (see the illustrations).

Bract — A small, modified, often pigmented leaf usually situated at the base of flowers or flower clusters.

Bulb — A thickened, fleshy structure that usually forms below ground and functions in food storage and reproduction (as an onion bulb).

Capsule — A fruit that dries and splits open at maturity, shedding its seeds; usually it contains two or more compartments.

Grasp — To appear to grasp the stem as some leaf blades that partly or totally encircle the stem.

Community — A group of organisms (plants) living together in a given habitat.

Coniferous — Adjectival form of conifer (a cone-bearing, usually evergreen gymnosperm).

Cushion — A form of growth (growth habit) of some plants, dense and low in stature, resembling a cushion.

Deciduous — Falling away, as leaves falling off at the end of the growing season.

Disk flower — One of the central flowers of a head of a sunflower, daisy, etc.; a tubular-shaped flower lacking a flattened extension (ray) (see the illustrations).

Dissemination — The act of spreading or scattering, such as seeds or pollen in the wind.

Dominant — One of the most important plants of a given community because of numbers and/or size; a plant which has a major effect on other plants of the community.

Elliptical — Longer than wide with similar ends (not egg-shaped); a squashed circle.

Elongate — Much longer than wide.

Fleshy — Rather thick and succulent; containing juices (water).

Flexuous — Limber, easily bent.

Follicle — A dry, pod-like fruit with a single compartment that splits open at maturity.

Gymnosperm — A seed-producing plant that lacks an ovary, for example, a conifer.

Glandular — Having glands that secrete resinous, often sticky material.

Glutinous — Covered by a sticky substance secreted through the epidermis.

Habitat — The home of a given plant, unique in having a particular set of environmental conditions.

Head — A dense cluster of flowers that lack stalks; the inflorescence of a composite or member of the sunflower family (see the illustrations).

Herb — A plant lacking a hard, woody stem.

Inferior — As related to an ovary: the flower parts borne on (above) the ovary or conversely, the ovary borne below (and inferior to) the flower parts (see the illustrations).

Inflorescence — A flower cluster.

Involucral bract — One of the bracts (reduced leaves) surrounding a flower head in the sunflower family, or below the umbrella-like inflorescence of the parsley family.

Irregular — Pertaining to a flower: bilaterally symmetrical.

Leaflet — One of the leaf-like segments of a compound leaf (see the illustrations).

Lithosol — Literally, rock-soil; a rocky, thin-soil habitat as in basaltic (lava-flow) areas.

Linear — Long and very narrow, with parallel sides.

Lobed — As applied to a leaf: cut or dissected (but not all the way to the midvein of the leaf).

Mat-forming — Low, dense, and spreading horizontally, resembling a mat or carpet.

Nocturnal — Active at night; as applied to flowers, open at night and closed during the day.

Nodding — As related to a flower: hanging with the face of the flower downward.

Nutlet — One of four or more small, hard-shelled, one-seeded fruits.

Oblong — Longer than wide.

Opposite — As related to leaves: paired at the nodes; two leaves per node (see the illustrations).

Ovary — The seed-containing part of the flower; the part of the flower that matures into a fruit (see the illustrations).

Ovate — Egg-shaped.

Palmate — Shaped like the palm of the hand with extended fingers.

Palmately compound — As applied to leaves: divided to the midvein in such a way that the leaflets are borne at the same point and spread like fingers (see the illustrations).

Pappus — Bristle-like or scale-like appendages borne on the ovary/fruit of members of the sunflower family; modified sepals. The pappus often functions in seed dispersal.

Parasite — Growing on and deriving nourishment from another living plant.

Pedicel — The stalk to a flower or fruit.

Perennial — A plant that lives more than two years; it may die down to the roots each year but sprouts up the next.

Petal — One of the bract-like segments of the inner-whorl of flower parts, usually colored or showy (see the illustrations).

Petiole — Leaf stalk (see the illustrations).

Pinnate — Feather-like, with a central axis and perpendicular projections; usually applied to a leaf.

Pinnately compound — As applied to leaves; divided to the midvein with the leaflet arranged on both sides of the extended axis of the petiole (see the illustrations).

Pistil — The central (female) part of the flower containing the ovary, style, and stigma (see the illustrations).

Pubescence — General term for hairiness, woolliness, etc.

Raceme — An elongate, unbranched flower cluster, each flower having a stalk or pedicel (see the illustrations).

Ray — The blade-like extension of a ray flower (see the illustrations).

Ray flower — One of the outer flowers of a sunflower, daisy, etc. that has a flattened, elongate, colorful extension (see the illustrations).

Receptacle — The tip of a flowering stalk (petiole) on which the parts of a flower are borne.

Regular — As related to a flower: radially symmetrical (see the illustrations).

Rhizome — An underground stem that produces roots and upright branches (stems); an organ by which plants (such as quack grass and Canadian thistle) spread.

Rootcrown — The juncture between the root and stem; the crown of the root.

Rootstalk — A rhizome.

Runner — A prostrate stem which roots at the nodes and produces erect branches (as with strawberries).

Saline — Salty, having sodium salts, potassium salts, etc.

Sepal — One of the bract-like segments of the outer whorl of flower parts, usually green (see the illustrations).

Sessile — Without a stalk; for example, leaf blades borne directly on the stem without a stalk are said to be sessile.

Shrub — A woody plant that branches at or near ground level.

Spike — An elongate flower cluster with sessile (non-stalked) flowers.

Spur — A hollow extension of a petal or sepal, often containing nectar.

Stamen — The pollen-containing part of the flower (see the illustrations).

Steppe — A non-forested region dominated by grasses and low shrubs.

Stigma — The pollen-receptive part of the pistil (see the illustrations).

Stipule — Leaf-like or bract-like appendage at the base of the petioles of some leaves. Stipules occur in pairs (see the illustrations).

Style — The narrow portion of the pistil, connecting the ovary with the pollen-receptive stigma (see the illustrations).

Succulent — Soft and juicy, filled with water.

Superior — As applied to an ovary: the flower parts borne on the receptacle below the ovary (see the illustrations); conversely, the ovary above (superior) to the other flower parts.

Talus — Loose gravel or boulders on a slope.

Taproot — An elongate, unbranched, vertical (carrot-like) root.

Umbel — An umbrella-shaped flower cluster or inflorescence (see the illustrations).

Unisexual — flowers (or plants) of one sex, either staminate (male) or pistilate (female).

Whorl — A group of three or more leaves, flowers, petals, or whatever, radiating from a single point such as a node (see the illustrations).

Woodland — An area dominated by widely spaced trees of low stature, savanna-like.

Xeric — Relating to dry or arid, for example, xeric habitat.

Cross Reference of Scientific and Common Names
(with page numbers in parentheses)

Index to Scientific Names
(boldface numbers are pages of photographs)

Index to Common Names
(boldfaced numbers are pages of photographs)

About the Author

Ronald J. Taylor was born in southeastern Idaho on the edge of sagebrush country, and he has never strayed far from its wide-open spaces. The author of numerous scientific and popular articles, Taylor has also written five books, including *Northwest Weeds*, published by Mountain Press. He now lives in Bellingham, Washington, where he teaches biology at Western Washington University.